WILLIAM ASBURY DODGE

SOUTHERN HOLINESS PIONEER

Compiled by

Kenneth O. Brown, Ph.D.

HOLINESS STUDIES SERIES
NUMBER FOUR

Published by
Holiness Archives
Hazleton, PA
2001

ISBN 0-9663403-5-3

Dr. Kenneth O. Brown
243 S. Pine Street
Hazleton, PA 18201

Printed by
COUNTRY PINES PRINTING
SHOALS, IN 47581
USA

CONTENTS

Dedication

Photographs

DEDICATION

This volume is dedicated to my dear friends, Joe and Marilyn Luce. They have given their lives to the service of others and the ministry of the holiness movement, especially the Indian Springs Holiness Camp Meeting. Joe Luce served as president of this encampment from 1990 to 2000.

Rev. William A. Dodge

Mrs. W. A. Dodge

W. A. Dodge with Mr. Benson and Mr. Fargo, the first camp ground keeper

Dodge Memorial

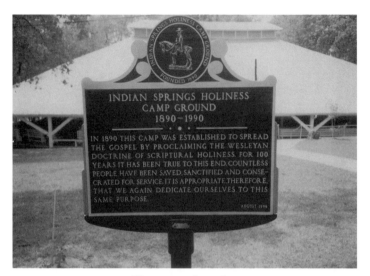

Close-up of marker

The Main Gate

INTRODUCTION

In 1876, after reading some of the writings of Mrs. Phoebe Palmer and other holiness leaders, Methodist pastor William A. Dodge made a complete consecration of his life to God, and claimed by faith the blessing of entire sanctification. Within five years he became one of the key leaders of the holiness movement in the South.

Over the last twenty years scholars have taken a renewed interest in the holiness revival and its impact upon the American religious landscape. Only recently, however, has that interest begun to focus on the South, and its contribution to the holiness cause. The South boosted the burgeoning holiness revival in numerous ways, and mention must be made of the southern camp meetings, mission organizations, schools and periodicals. But the most important southern contribution was its leadership, and preachers such as Sam Jones, William B. Godbey, Beverly Carradine, Henry C. Morrison, John L. Brasher and Bishop Joseph S. Key immediately come to mind.

In the limelight of that southern holiness leadership, one must also consider William A. Dodge. He was one of the moving spirits behind the founding of the Georgia Holiness Association in 1883, and served as the editor of its periodical. His evangelistic ministry took him to churches and camp meetings in numerous southern states, and the Midwest. Convinced of the importance and value of the holiness camp meetings, in 1890 he helped found the Indian Springs Holiness Camp Meeting near Flovilla, Georgia.

Several significant new studies on the holiness movement in the South have appeared, and most of these mention W. A. Dodge. Unfortunately, no new biographical study of his life has been written. Therefore, this new reprint edition is offered in honor and tribute to his life and work, and the important contributions he made to the southern holiness revival.

In order to assist those who would continue to study the life of this tireless worker, I have included in this volume several items of interest:

1. a picture of Reverend and Mrs. Dodge;
2. his conference memoir;
3. his obituary as it appeared in the *Pentecostal Herald*;
4. a copy of his handwritten consecration;
5. a copy of his article, "The Holiness Movement in the South," from the *Pentecostal Herald*;
6. an obituary of Mrs. Dodge; and
7. a select bibliography of materials.

PROLOGUE

The Reverend William Asbury Dodge served as a southern Methodist preacher for more than forty years, and ranks as one of the premier southern holiness leaders of the nineteenth century.

Born in Columbia County, Georgia, on September 30, 1844, William grew up in a Methodist home and became a Christian before his fourteenth birthday. He received his preacher's license on his seventeenth birthday, and entered the ministry of the Georgia Annual Conference of the Methodist Episcopal Church, South, in 1862. After serving as a chaplain in the Confederate army in 1864-1865, he returned to the pastorate, and in 1869 Bishop Holland McTyeire ordained him as elder. That same year he married Mary Etta [Jones] Chandler, widow of a Methodist minister who died while serving as a chaplain in the Confederate army. To their home came four children, one of whom died in infancy.

William A. Dodge rose in the ministerial ranks so rapidly that in just three years he received appointment as the Presiding Elder (District Superintendent) of the Dahlonega District. Following that he served one year as Presiding Elder of the Gainesville District, and in 1875-1876 served as pastor of the large St. Paul's Methodist Episcopal Church, South, in Atlanta, where he again claimed by faith the experience of entire sanctification.

Dodge had professed the experience of holiness on two previous occasions, the first time in 1870 while he ministered at Evans Chapel in Atlanta, and again in 1873 when he served as Presiding Elder. Unhappily, he lost the experience both times, largely due to lack of faith. In 1875, when he again moved to Atlanta, a friend introduced him to some popular holiness literature, including the writings of Mrs. Phoebe Palmer and a southern periodical entitled *Way of Holiness*. This paper, founded in 1871 by William Baker as the *Southern Methodist Home Altar,* was the first holiness periodical published in the South. This literature again encouraged Dodge to seek the experience of holiness. On April 15, 1876, during a revival service in his church, he implored his people to join him in "seeking the blessing," and about a dozen persons met with him in his study for prayer. This impromptu gathering lasted about an hour, and then the people went home. Dodge continued to pray alone, however, until he finally decided to write out his consecration, which he called "a written deed of myself to God, with all I had."

Atlanta, Ga., April 15, 1876

I this day make a full consecration of all I have to God. Now, henceforth, forever. Myself, my body, eyes, tongue, hands, feet, mind and heart. My wife, Mary Dodge; my boy, Wesley Atticus Dodge, and my little daughter, Mae Belle Dodge, my books, clothes, money, all I now have. Yes, all my means are, and shall be, Thine. My time, and if there is anything else that appertains to me, that I have not mentioned, I lay it on the altar to stay there forever. I do this from a conviction of duty—that all I have belongs by right to Him. Not as a compromise, but from a sense of duty, simply asking that I may be aided by Him to keep it there. Signed, sealed and delivered in the study of St. Paul's Church, Atlanta, Ga., April 15, 1876, in the presence of Him who sees all things, with the Spirit to witness.

(Signed) W. A. Dodge

After he penned these words, Dodge placed the written consecration in an envelope, and it remained sealed until 1904. His family found the document among his other papers in an old trunk after he died. Having made the consecration, Dodge began to ask the Lord to come and accept the offering he had made. He later wrote,

On…the day following, in the study of the church, about half-past twelve o'clock, I felt that God sent His fire and consumed the offering. I felt that He went through me and cleansed my poor soul from all sin, and oh! what views I had of Jesus, such as I never had before.

Shortly after this the revival in Dodge's church took on new momentum, and by the end of April he had received thirty-five new members. Furthermore, Dodge became settled and established in his new experience, and began to preach holiness to his congregation with the fervor of a revivalist.

In the winter of 1880 northern evangelist John S. Inskip, president of the National Camp Meeting Association for the Promotion of Holiness, held holiness revival meetings in five southern cities, including Augusta, Georgia. Shortly after the Augusta meeting, Dodge and fellow Methodist pastor, Anderson J. Jarrell, met and discussed methods of promoting the holiness cause in the Georgia Annual Conference. Following a district function, Dodge and Jarrell met with a small group of interested persons, and the group decided to conduct annual holiness conventions. By 1882 they decided to publish a periodical, with Dodge as editor, and named it *Tongue of Fire*. In 1883 twenty-four ministers and nearly one hundred laypersons from both Georgia conferences met in Gainsville, Georgia, and formally organized the "Georgia Holiness Association," with A. J. Jarrell as president. Within a few months, they changed the name of the paper to *Way of Life*. In the spring of 1885 the association decided to form a separate organization for the southern part of the state, and officially organized the "South Georgia Holiness Association," with Joseph S. Key as its first president. Key was elected Bishop in 1886.

Dodge worked tirelessly for the cause of holiness in Georgia, sometimes traveling into other states to secure workers for their city mission activities. He supported the National Camp Meeting held in Augusta, Georgia, in 1885, as did fellow pastor, Clement Anselm Evans, former general in the Confederate Army. The Augusta encampment won many hundreds of persons to the holiness cause, but some tactless remarks by George Douglas Watson and William McDonald planted seed that soon hurt the movement, and brought brutal ecclesiastical chastisement upon its followers. Few felt the effects of those blows more than Dodge. In 1885 he served a large and important parish on the Gainesville District, but two years later he rode a rural circuit in Fulton County. In 1889 he who had twice served as a district superintendent received appointment as the junior preacher at Walker Street Methodist

Episcopal Church, South, in Atlanta. Finally, in 1894, the powers that be appointed Dodge as a city missionary in Atlanta, the same position he had served twenty years before.

Fortunately for southern Methodism, William A. Dodge was not trying to climb the corporate ladder. He could not be run off, nor would he quit under adverse conditions. A power higher than a Methodist Bishop controlled his life, and he adamantly refused to leave the church, or lead people away from the Methodist fold. He submitted his pastoral ministry to the authority of the Methodist Episcopal Church, South, and at the same time held true to his convictions about the doctrine of entire sanctification. Because of this he stood as one of the great stabilizing forces of the holiness movement in the South.

Over the years Dodge became one of the most effective southern holiness leaders and revivalists. He ministered at the conventions of the Georgia Holiness Association, and preached at holiness camp meetings in Georgia and several other states. In 1889 he, along with H. A. Hodges, J. H. Curry and George W. Matthews picked out the location for a permanent camp meeting as the home of the Georgia Holiness Association. The leaders conducted the first session of the Indian Springs Holiness Camp Meeting in 1890, and it quickly became the flagship of southern holiness encampments, attracting thousands of visitors over the years. Dodge loved the Indian Springs Holiness Camp Meeting and gave the last thirteen years of his life to its ministry. He is considered as one of its founders.

Late in 1903, Dodge became seriously ill. On January 16, 1904, realizing that his end was near, he called his wife and children to his side for a final embrace and prayers. His wife asked him if he felt that the Lord Jesus was still with him. He promptly said, "Yes, and He has been with me all the time." At 4:00 that afternoon, William A. Dodge died peacefully in his home. His funeral was held the following Monday at Walker Street Methodist Episcopal Church, South, in Atlanta, where he had formerly served as pastor. Hundreds of persons crowded into the building for the service, and George W. Matthews preached the funeral sermon.

REV. W. A. DODGE

As We Knew Him

WITH

SKETCHES OF HIS LIFE, DIARY, CONSECRATION AND SERMONS

———

Compiled by
MRS. J. WM. GARBUTT.

———

ATLANTA, GA.
The Franklin Printing and Publishing Company
Geo. W. Harrison, Manager.
1906

DEDICATION

TO THE GLORY OF GOD, AND TO THE DEAR ONES LEFT BEHIND

BY THAT FATHER IN ISRAEL, REV. W. A. DODGE,

THIS VOLUME IS DEDICATED

BY THE COMPILER,

MRS. S. S. GARBUTT,

WRIGHT, GA.,

JUNE 22, 1906

TABLE OF CONTENTS.

PREFACE.

Having waited two full years for some more facile pen, some erudite brother who had known the subject of these sketches longer and far better than it had been my happy lot to know him, and yet feeling unwilling that a life so noble, a character so grand, a heart so pure, and an ever-dominant purpose so great in all, and through all, to glorify God, and not having heard of such intention on the part of any one, after much prayer, I seemed to catch from heavenly realms, woman though I be, an inspiration to attempt the things myself.

For it seemed meet that some one should set forth more fully than had hitherto been done, the things that W. A. Dodge "began both to do and to teach," that we, our children, and children's children might hear, know and remember thereof.

To many brethren and some sisters I am indebted for most of the subject-matter, very much of which remains unchanged.

Asking your prayers that God will use it, in His own way, to bless the world, the Church and "The Holiness Movement," I am,

Yours for all that is good,

Mrs. S. S. Garbutt.

Wright, Ga., May 29, 1906.

DODGE MEMORIAL HALL.

The proceeds of the sale of this Book are to be applied to the erection of this Cottage at Indian Spring Campmeeting, for the entertainment of Preachers.

INTRODUCTION.

It is with sincere pleasure I take my pen to write a few introductory words to these sketches.

Brother Dodge stands in my spiritual memory gallery, first of all, as

A BROTHER BELOVED.

Greater still than a preacher, greater than a warrior for the faith, it is to be a "brother"—one yoked in love to every other minister and witness of full salvation—a brother bound by tenderest ties of love to every one that misunderstood or opposed the doctrine he taught. A brother, too, to every man for whom Christ died, even if in rags, or chains and sin, and a brother indeed of the helping, giving kind, and not simply the sort who profess much and do little. Christ's perfect love in him made him a real lover of men, and I shall never know him as "Doctor," but rather as "Brother Dodge."

Next, his memory stands before my affection's eye as a full-length portrait of

A MAN FILLED WITH THE HOLY GHOST.

Besides the character traits, there are certain outward marks which follow such a man in any generation.

Here are two of them: First, a high appreciation on the part of the spiritually-minded; and, second, a

severe depreciation on the part of the worldly-minded
within and without the church.   Brother Dodge
wore both of these marks.

As it was with Stephen, so it was with him—
"They chose him" because he was a man "full of
faith and the Holy Ghost."   And for the very same
cause, "they (the other they) stoned him."

Justly beloved and unjustly discounted are the
crown and the battle-scars with which the witnesses
of the Spirit pass through this world to their home.

Thirdly, he next appears to me

AS A PREACHER,

preaching the highest things in the gospel, and he
always did it in the humblest way.   Never without
"bread" and "fishes" in his basket, he knew, however, that it would take a big blessing on these to
make them go round.   So he spoke simply, and trusted implicitly in the Holy Spirit.   He explained, em-
phasized, enforced, and ensampled the doctrine and
experience of "perfect love."

He disentangled holiness from many other things,
good, bad and indifferent, which misinformed persons and confused thinkers mixed with it, at its expense, and to its hurt, and he distinguished it clearly
from other teachings concerning the Spirit which
leaves unsolved the problem of sin in the human
heart.

One such life and ministry silences a thousand
voices which tell of no better sanctification than
merely a covering for sin, and proves the promise

.true that God will cleanse us from all our idols and filthiness, and that peace as a river and righteousness as the waves of the sea might be continually manifest in the heart and life.

No more fitting monument could be erected to Brother Dodge's ministry than some "upper room" lodge at the Indian Spring camp-meeting which he loved so well, where his brethren in the ministry might tarry to light their torches from the Pentecostal blaze, and go forth "to spread scriptural holiness over these lands."

JOSEPH H. SMITH.

Redlands, California, June 25, 1906.

REV. W. A. DODGE'S CONSECRATION IN 1876.

Atlanta, Ga., April 15, 1876.

I this day make a full consecration of all I have to God. Now, henceforth, forever. Myself, my body, eyes, tongue, hands, feet, mind and heart.

My wife, Mary Dodge; my boy, Wesley Atticus Dodge, and my little daughter, Mae Belle Dodge, my books, clothes, money, all I now have, and all I ever expect to have. Yes, all my means are, and shall be thine. My time, and if there is anything else that appertains to me, that I have not mentioned, I lay it on the altar to stay there forever.

I do this from a conviction of duty—that all I have belongs by right to Him. Not as a compromise, but from a sense of duty, simply asking that I may be aided by Him to keep it there.

Signed, sealed and delivered in the study of St. Paul's Church, Atlanta, Ga., April 15, 1876, in the presence of Him who sees all things, with the Spirit to witness.

(Signed),   W. A. DODGE.

Several months after Brother Dodge went to the good world, the above "consecration" was found written on a sheet of paper, in an old trunk in which he kept valuable papers.

On the envelope enclosing it, after it had been sealed, he wrote the following directions:

"This is to stay sealed during my natural life, being the instrument of my 'consecration' to God."

　(Signed),　　　　　　　　　W. A. DODGE.

A BRIEF TRIBUTE.

I regret very much that I am unable to contribute anything of general interest to the memorial of Brother Dodge. His loyalty to his church and the great cause of Scriptural Holiness, so clearly taught in the Bible, and expounded in her standards, challenged my admiration, while his lovable character elicited my warmest affection. I know that you will regret to learn that even if I had the material at hand, I am physically unable to put it in shape for the press. With love I am,

　　Your brother in Christ,

　　　　　　　　W.W. TURNER.

LaGrange, Ga., June 7, 1906.

Arouse! Arouse!! dear friend, before it be eternally too late. Make sure you are saved, and remember that the Gospel alone is the power of God unto salvation.

THE EARLY LIFE OF REV. W. A. DODGE.

W. A. Dodge's boyhood gave small promise of the great future to which he attained, and there was little indication of the intense zeal that characterized his life under the baptism of the Holy Ghost.

There was will-power among his native gifts, and there was decision of character there, and honesty of purpose, integrity and truth; a cheerful and happy spirit, coupled sometimes with more or less of innocent fun and mischief, which were part and parcel of his nature. His devotion to his mother was beautiful to look upon. These were some of the basic elements of his character; and when touched and taught by the hand of God, each helped to make a man of him.

When he was seven years old his father died, and his mother, with four small children, Asbury the oldest, moved back to the home of her father, John Mercer. There little Asbury worked on the farm and attended a country school, as he had opportunity, desiring to prepare himself to be of some service to his mother in her needs. The responsibility put upon him at this early age was a potent factor in the development of his character.

His hard work on the farm contributed also to developing him physically, and he grew out of a lubberly boy into a man of large physical stature. This field of industry, moreover, was excellent training for the character which would be called upon in the future to surmount obstacles.

The influence of adverse circumstances in making men is a potent, palpable factor. Lincoln owed much to the humble log cabin in which he was reared, and also to the muscular exertion required at the hands of the young frontiersman in felling forests and splitting rails. Garfield was born in poverty, and had a sore conflict for existence, until, as a young teacher, he got a start in the world for the noble career of usefulness, which landed him in the White House.

And Asbury Dodge, plodding his weary way behind the plow, was accumulating strength and gathering wisdom necessary for the stern conflicts of life into which he was afterward thrown. Where there was work to do, he freely gave himself to the task. Young as he was, he had his mother to lean on him as her prop and stay in the absence of a loving father.

Nor was he less devoted to his grandparents. After he grew up and became a member of the North Georgia Conference he never failed to make them a visit at the close of each session of his Conference, unless he was providentially hindered. Money was scarce at such times as this, but "I must see grandma," he would say out of his great big heart, larger even than his finely-formed body.

He appreciated no little the meager advantages of the country school to which he was sent in the few weeks which he could snatch in the intervals between hard work; and while he did not signalize his school

days by any special brilliancy, he was laying well
the foundations of a thoughtful, settled, solid character. It is remarkable that so many great and good
men, while in school, have given so little indication
of the wide sphere of usefulness which they were intended to fill.

Sir Walter Scott was a notoriously dull boy while
in school, nor could a single one of his teachers have
predicted at that time his future place in the very
front ranks of English literature; and Dr. Adam
Clark was regarded by his tutors as a very unpromising boy, and yet he developed, later on, into one of
the most learned men of his day, and a standard au-
thor in early Methodism.

Asbury Dodge, with the helping agency of the old
field school was to develop not only mentally, but
spiritually, and immortally.

Under the guidance of Mrs. McCormick, a saintly
woman, who more than fifty years ago organized a
Sunday-school at old Linwood Church, in Columbia
county, and who continued in charge of it for over
forty years, young Dodge was soundly converted.
He said "the sky never looked so blue, and the stars
never shined so bright as they did that night," when
he passed from death unto life.

This glorious fact in his history changed the whole
current of his character and life. An interesting and
impressive incident is related of him about that time.

His grandfather permitted a negro boy named
Perry to go with him to church, three miles from
home. They rode the same horse. Asbury was con-

verted, and when they started home after the service, immediately he began to preach to his colored companion, "O Perry, give your heart to God! O Perry, give your heart to God!" and all the way home he kept it up, shouting with all his might, and preaching the gospel to his colored congregation, while Perry was weeping and praying, and crying for mercy.

If he had been called later on to be a missionary in the heart of Africa, or to go to the jungles of India, he would have rivalled Robert Moffatt, or equaled David Livingstone in zeal, faith and fidelity to God, and in his unwearied efforts to save souls.

His grandmother rejoiced with him over his conversion, saying she hoped that the Lord would call "Buddie" (as she called him) to preach the gospel, and the hope was fully realized, as we well know.

He was licensed to exhort just as he reached his sixteenth birthday, and was licensed to preach on his seventeenth birthday. In 1862 he joined the old Georgia Conference, and from that time his life was wholly that of an itinerant Methodist preacher.

Bishop Haygood, then Presiding Elder of the Athens District, took him in hand and sent him as a supply to the Watkinsville circuit. Asbury had a meeting at Watkinsville, and after the Presiding Elder had preached Asbury asked the congregation to meet him at sundown and have secret prayer out in the grove. The Presiding Elder said, when he got to the church in time to preach that night, he heard Asbury Dodge praying half a mile away, and begging God to come down and be with them that night, and God did come in mighty power, and they had the best meeting he ever saw. But Asbury entirely forgot at the time he was *praying in secret*.

Blessed man! He lived for the glory of God and the good of others; always ready to go where there was anything to do for his Master, or where he could comfort and help His suffering people. He never knew how to spare himself. He was one of the best nurses among the sick of his own family or the families of his neighbors. For three weeks' he waited on Rev. Dr. Lovick Pierce in his last sickness in Sparta, Ga., sleeping in his room every night for that long time. Just before the old Doctor died he said to him, "Tell Sister Dodge I am trespassing on the General Rules of the Church—borrowing without any probability of paying," referring to the very free use he made of her devoted husband.

But they are together now. "Not dead, but sleepeth."

THOMAS A. SEALS,

North Georgia Conference.

"O sacred union with the Perfect Mind!
Transcendent bliss, which thou alone canst give,
How blest are they, this pearl of price who find,
And, dead to earth, have learned in Thee to live.

A MAN OF PRAYER.

Brother W. A. Dodge was a man of prayer. That which was conspicuous in his life was the prayer habit. It was his rule to pray—this was his business, viz., to pray. Duty as well as habit compelled him to pray. In the morning, rising from sleep, he invariably knelt and gave thanks to God, and thus he sanctified the bed, the night, the awakening, and the coming day by prayer.

It would scarcely be decent, surely not manly, not to be at prayer before going out of the sleeping chamber. Morning and night his home was buttressed by public praise and family prayer, in which every one in the home took part. Never too busy, never too late indulging in sleep, never too much in haste, for prayer.

The home runs to disorder and confusion without prayer. The world fills the home that is not filled with prayer. Sin stains the home that is not washed by prayer.

A preacher he was, and, of course, he had family prayers, night and morning! A shame for him not to do this family praying, but there are many preachers who do not thus call upon God.

Prayer was his strong resource in time of trouble. Any one going wrong, any one sick, trials or troubles of any kind, if not with us, we knew where to find him. We knew that he was praying, somewhere. "When Brother Dodge visited our home he

always made it a rule to pray before he left, and he
talked with the Lord in such a way that it left no
doubt he was personally acquainted with Him,"
writes Brother Charlie D. Tillman.

Brother Huckabee, of Texas, says he was with
Brother Dodge one night and half a day at a Convention. When the brethren called upon him,
Brother Dodge prayed with them before they left.
Brothers Dodge and Huckabee were together in
prayer three different times during that night and
half-day.

There was a great reunion of the Dodge family
in Salem, Mass., in 1879, and Hon. W. E. Dodge,
of New York, was president. Brother W. A. Dodge
was the one selected to pray, to give thanks and in-
voke God's blessings. One present said that "it
was characteristic of the Dodge family to call upon
the Lord for assistance in all their acts—that the
Dodge family was an honored, heroic, God-serving
race."

Brother Dodge was a prayerful man, which means
more than a man of prayer. The habit only, conscience alone, duty and training, may make us men
who pray. But the praying may be the merest habit,
an onerous duty-doing, a sheer performance, a dead,
dull thing, a sham, a delusion, a hypocrisy. The
Pharisees were men of prayer, but a prayerful man
is one whose whole life has been toned, sweetened,
refined, sanctified by prayer. The essence of prayer
has gone into his life and affected his character.

The prayerful man "prays without ceasing." The

fragrance of prayer always surrounds him, the spirit of prayer is always with him. His soul is constantly in the attitude of looking up to God. The prayerful man is ever talking with God, ever breathing out his soul after God, and ever communing with God. To him the sun of prayer never sets, nor does the light of prayer ever withdraw itself. Brother Dodge had been in the fountain when the angel of prayer was there, and his life and spirit and character had the healing incident to that blessed occasion. He realized the power of prayer, and illustrated his faith by his praying.

His little girl, now grown into womanhood, was once sick unto death with pneumonia. The Doctor stayed by her bed for ten days. While praying for the child and earnestly asking God to show him what would relieve her, it was deeply impressed on his mind to give her water, which she had not been willing or able to drink during her sickness. He began administering it by moistening her lips, and then by draughts, oft repeated, and she began to amend at once. This but illustrated the simple, the strong, the child-like faith of this man of prayer.

Bishop Soule, when dying, was asked by Bishop McTyeire: "Are you praying?" The answer came quickly and emphatically: "Not now." The praying time was over—the praying was all done.

So with Brother Dodge, there came a time when he did not pray to live. At the hospital, two weeks before his death, his wife said, "Mr. Dodge, why don't you ask God to cure you?" "Darling," he replied, "I believe that God wants me to go now. I have prayed for Him to spare me till the children were grown and settled, He has answered my prayer, and I believe that he wants me to go now."

Brother W. A. Dodge is dead, but his earnest prayers are vocal and potent. He has left to us the rich legacy of his prayers. The richest inheritance the world can have are the prayers of a holy man. They are immortal, never-dying, and priceless in value.

E. M. BOUNDS.

Washington, Ga., June 15, 1906.

THIS MAN KNEW HOW TO PRAY.

Some years since the eldest daughter of Rev. Sam Jones was dangerously ill in Cartersville, Ga., and her life was despaired of. Brother Jones and wife were greatly distressed, but they believed in the God who answers prayer. Telegrams were sent to various persons known to have power with God, and one went in haste to W. A. Dodge, Atlanta, to "pray for Mary, she is near death's door." This man of prayer readily responded, and to the surprise of many the young woman recovered. To this day Brother and Sister Jones believe that the deliverance was wrought through the prayers of Christians, one of whom was Brother Dodge.

A PREACHER AND TEACHER.

How different the view of the Christian with regard to life, its duties and happiness, from that of the world! The one says, fortune, fame, happiness. The other says, duty to God and man, however humble the sphere, brings success in its highest sense, and happiness as a moral sequence—happiness for the soul and peace for the mind. The baubles of fame and fortune are not to be taken into the account by the child of God.

Brother W. A. Dodge's life was a success in the sphere of a philanthropist, and went further by reaching the spiritual. He had the advantage that many have not, of being well born, and properly reared, and, as a natural result, gave his heart and life to God in the days of his youth.

The writer's first acquaintance with him was in 1862. He was then junior preacher on the Watkinsville circuit, and only eighteen years old, but had at that time that same Christian zeal and religious energy which ever afterward characterized his life.

In his youthful ministry he gave promise of the success and usefulness that grew with age and time, and long before the angels came for him he was a well-matured Christian gentleman.

If he ever backslid from his first love, I never heard him mention it. He lived on the plane, all the time, where entire sanctification begins. After many years of a useful ministry on circuit, station, and as

THE TONGUE OF FIRE.

PUBLISHED WEEKLY.　　　　"FIRST PURE—THEN MATURE."　　　　75 CENTS A YEAR

VOL. II.　　　　ATLANTA, GA., SEPTEMBER 22, 1883.　　　　NO. 20

Entered as second class matter in the post office at Atlanta, Ga.

The Gospel Song.

BY MRS. MINNIE CALDWELL.

Tune—"I Know that My Redeemer Liveth."

Behold the Lamb! much loved of God,
. Slain for our sins;
He bore for us the chastening rod.
. Remission wins.

Oh, that blood! that blood! that blood!
Was shed to set us free,
Oh, that blood! that blood!
It cleanseth me.

His blood, it was the precious price
Which paid our debt,
The all-atoning sacrifice,
. It cleanses yet.

And love impelled him from his throne
To suffer here,
The sins of all the world atone.
Then draw us near.

Come, then, by faith, and test the word,
God's power know:
And wash your garments in the blood;
Be white as snow.

Yes, come unite in one accord
To praise his name,
Extroll the mercy of our Lord,
Ever the same.

And as we stand before the throne
With praise and psalm,
We'll claim no merits of our own;
Saved by the Lamb!

EXPERIENCE.

Bro Dodge: I was converted 15 years ago. I enjoyed religion for two years, I attended class, prayer meetings and enjoyed religion as much as any justified man can. Satan put it into my head that I was called to preach, and I would not agree. And then for thirteen years I wandered in the wilderness, never satisfied concious, something was lacking. Did not know what it was until the holiness meeting was in Gainesville. About four years ago I began to practice a sin that continued up to the Holiness Meeting. Over this I had a hard struggle, the Spirit on one side and Satan on the other. And in the midst of this meeting, and my souls fight over this sin, I had a financial and a personal difficulty. I heard the holiness brethren relating their experience, and I said, I will seek Holiness. Then Satan came and said if you get Holiness you will have to go to China and preach. ! O, how my troubles grew, and by the minute the burden increased until I felt that I could not live

much longer.. So in my desperation I told the blessed Savior "I will go to China, or any where else preach or do anything else, if thou wilt only relieve me. And when I did surrender it did not take the Lord long to bless my soul, but I did not yet have holiness, the blessing I wanted, for I did not have faith to claim that I was sanctified entire. About three or four days after, I went out to the. woods all alone and after a long struggle I took Christ as my sanctification by simple faith without any feeling, for the feeling did not come for several days, but it did come, and it abides most of the time and now whether I have feeling or not, I have an abiding trust in Christ as my perfect and complete Savior.

R. H. S.

A Petition

Heavenly Father, give an ear to one, yes, even hear my feeble petition for I am going to ask something of thee, Lord thou hast been so good and merciful to me in the past, yes O Lord thou hast. I was a sinner and thou didst quicken and convert my poor soul, and made me to rejoice in thy love, but Lord at times I feel in my heart that I still have sin, a very abominable thing in thing in thy sight and I know that thou hast no pleasure in it. Lord I feel it and I know it and now, yes now, I ask thee to give me a heart cleansed from all sin, pride, envy, malice and everything Lord that is displeasing to thee. I do want a pure heart, one that can be held blameless until the coming of the day. Lord, hear me, my soul hungers with thirst after more of thy love.

I know I am not worthy of such a blessing Lord, but thou hast said, "if any man thirsts, let him come unto thee and drink," and "if ye shall ask anything in my name I will do it." I do ask this and I continue to ask, for thou hast said, "What things so ever ye desire, when ye pray, believe that ye receive them, and ye shall have them."

Lord, I have asked and thou knowest I desire it above all things. What more can I do? What must I do? Believe, yes, thank the Lord I do believe, I do believe. Praise his holy name. _ All nations say

praise his holy name, holy name. The angels in heaven say praise his holy, holy name. Thank the Lord I, yes even I can praise his holy name. O Lord thou hast heard and filled my poor, poor heart; O why is it that all don't have this great prize for I know that thou art so ready and willing to fill any and all poor hungering and thirsting souls, that will only ask and believe on thy precious word. Here Lord I am, take me and use me as thou seest best, and continue to fill me with thy holy spirit.

O, Christ, to me thyself impart,
And reign unrivalled in my heart;
From this glad moment let me be,
Completely swallowed up in thee.

Where'er to thee my thoughts I raise,
I will adore thy wondrous grace;
Thy grace so vast, so rich, so free,
That reached to each and reached
o'er me.

O thee o'er all I gladly bring,
I rest beneath thy shadowing wing;
Since thou dost give thyself to me,
my heaven of love I find in thee.''

Fairmount, Geo.　A. E.

What is in Thine Hand?

What is in thine hand, Shamgar? An ox-goad with which I urge my lazy beasts. Use it for God; and Shamgar's ox-goad defeates the Philistines. What is in thine hand David? My sling, with which I keep the wolves from the sheep. Yet with that sling he slew Goliah, whom an army dare not meet. What is in thine hand disciple? Nothing but five barley loaves and two small fishes. Bring them to me —wive them to God; and the multitude is fed. What is inthine hand, poor widow? Only two mites. Give them to God; and behold! the fame of your riches fills the world. What hast thou, weeping woman? An alabaster box ` of ointment. Give it to God; break it, and pour it upon the Savior's head, and its sweet perfume is a fragrance in the church till now. What hast thou Dorcas? My needle. Use it for God; and these coats and garments keep multiplying, and are clothing the naked still! You are a manufacturer, or a merchant, or a mechanic, or a man of leisure, a lady of fortune, or a student, or a sewing woman. God wants each of you to serve him where you are. You have your business; use it for

God. Order it in a goodly manner. Do not allow any wickedness in it. Give goodly wages; preach Jesus to your clerks, not by a long face, but by being like him—doing good. Use your profits for God—feeding the hungry, clothing the naked, visiting the sick, comforting the wretched, spreading the gospel far and wide. Use your wealth, which is in your hand and as easily moved as the pen which gives your signature to keep that family in their home and to eject them. ?

What a field you have to glorify God in, just where you are. If you have nothing, use your tools for Him. He can glorify himself with them as easily as he could with a shepard's stick, an oxgoad, a sling, or two mites. A poor girl who had nothing but a sewing machine used it to aid a feeble church. All her earnings above her needs were given towards building a house of worship, and in a year she paid more than others a hundred times richer than she. So you can do if you will. Think of the widow with her two mites, the woman with the alabaster box, and Dorcas with her garments, You can do as much, and have a great reward.—[Free Church Record.

Our Proposition.

Timmons Proposition.
To give an aditional 75cts for the gratuitous circulation of the "Tongue of Fire." Responses.

Rev B. E. L. Timmons Calhoun Ga.,	75
Rev R. F. Evans, So. Ga. Conf,	1 25
Rev W. C. Dunlap Jonesboro Ga,	1 00
Rev E. B. Reese, Thomson Ga,	75
Mrs I. C. Dodge Macon Ga,	75
Rev. J. W. Lee, Dalton, `	75
Mrs. Mary J. Bowles, Macon, 1	00
Mrs. S. E. Carpenter, Blackshear,	75

Bro. F. A. Hall's Proposition to be one to give five dollars to raise one hundred dollars to circulate the Way of Life, has the following votes. ?

F. A. Hall, Milledgeville,	$ 5 00
Dr. G. P., S. C.,	10 00
J. M. Augusta,	5 00
J. C. F., Augusta,	5 00
John W. Wallace, Augusta,	5 00
A Sister,	5 00

Who will be the next?

presiding elder, he read the "Life of Carvosso," and was convicted for that blessing which he and all the other Methodist preachers who join the Conference, tell the Bishop they are going on unto, groaning after, and expect to attain to in this life. He sought it definitely and specifically, and obtained it as a second work of grace.

Since the entire sanctification of Dr. Lovick Pierce, Russell Reneau and Samuel Anthony, many years ago, there had been a lapse in the preaching and experience of full salvation, and Brother Dodge was one among the first to come under the revival of this Wesleyan, Scriptural doctrine, and from that happy period in his life the doctrine of holiness was the great theme of his heart and life, of his lips and pen.

This was the great secret of his power. It ran through all his charges like a current of salvation, and was that which thrilled and made happy many a pilgrim on his journey home, and which saved scores of souls from the power and dominion of sin.

Brother Dodge was the first one in our Conference after Dr. Pierce to enter the field with his pen to propagate this blessed experience, and Scriptural doctrine of full salvation. "The Way of Life," at first "The Tongue of Fire," which was a blessing to thousands of souls, was started by him. It was a little two-sheet affair in its beginning, but it grew and entered into five thousand homes, which undoubtedly represented that many readers, every week before it was merged into "The Kentucky Methodist," now "The Pentecostal Herald," of Louisville, Ky.

As a writer, Brother Dodge was pointed and pithy. He aimed at the heart, and always struck it. To sum it up—he was a kind and devoted husband, a loving father, a faithful and sympathetic pastor, a friend true and tried, a preacher full of zeal, of faith and of the Holy Ghost, remarkably gifted in prayer, and the best all-round camp-meeting preacher that I ever knew—the Saint John of the North Georgia Conference.

Farewell, my golden-hearted friend! Sing and shout on in that far-away, blissful clime, and we'll hail thee ere long in that land of eternal song. And when the awakening sound of the archangel's trumpet invades the death land my hope is to join you with the "one hundred and forty-four thousand," and the multitude that no man can number, who have washed their robes and made them white in the blood of the lamb. Amen!

E. G. MURRAH,

North Georgia Conference.

Macon, Ga.

AS A SPIRITUAL ADVISER OF CHRISTIAN WORKERS.

About 1885 I became acquainted with Brother Dodge through "The Way of Life," which was such a blessing to thousands of people in the years of its existence.

As I would read this paper, I saw there was a great and good man at its head. He was kind enough to print my first newspaper article, which was the experience of a green, awkward boy, just reclaimed, who mistook it for sanctification, and I was the boy.

The influence of "The Way of Life," as well as of its editor, will ever abide. In the meetings in which I now engage, I can now and then hear an experience dating back to the reading of "The Way of Life."

After I was married and moved to Atlanta, about 1892, it was our good fortune to live neighbor to this man of God. I was often in his office, and he always took time to talk with me.

Let me say here, those were my first days in the "song book" business. At that time Brother Dodge held a controlling interest in a song book, "Golden Harp," and he was in position to push its sale through "The Way of Life," and was just then beginning to have a good sale. Years afterward he told me that he saw I was desirous to come on into the field of song, and rather than compete with a young brother who seemed to have some promise, he quietly withdrew, and the sale of "Golden Harp" was no longer pushed.

I do not know how this impresses the reader, but it makes the writer feel like that his own stock of religion at this point is very low. This, and many other things in the life of this man, better known to ourselves than to others, have been of untold value to me.

His advice was always safe. More than once I have been in doubt as to certain business ventures which looked a little questionable, and I would have no trouble in deciding what to do after I had talked with Brother Dodge.

He was my pastor for a year at Walker Street Church, Atlanta, and for four years at East Point. Some people accused us of following him, and I may say it is no great concern if they thought so. Pastors who knew him best would not blame us for doing so.

Just at this time the weight of immortal souls began to grow upon me, and Brother Dodge was ever ready to encourage me, and even let me try to preach at some of his appointments. It was no wonder that I followed him. His words of cheer and hearty "amens" would make a little fellow feel like he was saying something, whether he was or not. Preachers who read this know just what I am talking about, and they would have done just as I did.

If I ever do anything in preaching (and the Lord has helped me hold some good meetings, where scores have been saved), I will always give the credit to

Brother Dodge and my sainted father, who were so patient with and helpful to me years ago. Praise be unto God for help that comes just at the right time!

As a pastor, he endeared himself to us all. He was in our home often before and after our first child came, and so much did his prayers and talks impress us, we counted it a privilege to honor the baby with his name. We could think of nothing so suitable to couple with it as Jewel. So our first born bears the name of Jewel Dodge. She was baptized by Brother Dodge at Indian Spring camp-ground when about five months old. We have always felt that with such a name she can not afford to do anything displeasing to our Heavenly Father. Brother Dodge was our pastor when three other little ones were born to us, and we shall always feel grateful to God that they ever had the hands of this man on their heads in holy baptism, as we brought them to Him in consecration. We are praying that they may live so as to meet him in heaven.

His visits to our home were always a benediction, and helpful in many ways. His information on general subjects seemed unlimited. He was posted on the best methods of conducting a successful farm and everything in connection with it, as well as the best methods of conducting a charge and everything connected with it. Many things will be seen from others' pens in this book which will show what he was as a pastor.

His association on the road while on the way to meetings was a blessing to me. One of our trips together to be remembered was to Scottsville, Texas, where, through his influence, I did my first work in that holiness camp. (I have been there two or three times since.) As soon as we arrived I could see how much was thought of Brother Dodge. Even the little children, who had heard their fathers and mothers talk about him, were eager to see him. I soon felt at home there; for all that anybody cared to know was that Brother Dodge said, "He is safe; let him do what he wants to," and they did. (You understand, Brother Dodge was one who helped to establish Scottsville camp-ground.) On these trips we would room together and eat and sleep together, and I was a better man by it.

Let me say something of his home life, something I suppose which will not be known unless I tell it. Here is one little incident to show his wonderful control of disturbances among children. Once when there was a misunderstanding between his two little girls, and the excitement was growing to a very high pitch, being mixed with scratching and hair-pulling, their papa appeared on the scene, and began to sing in a sweet and melodious strain:

> "If we knew the baby fingers,
> Pressed against the window pane,
> Would be cold and still to-morrow,
> Ne'er to trouble us again;
> Would the bright eyes of our darling
> Catch the frown upon our brow?
> Would the print of rosy fingers,
> Vex us then as they do now?"

The disturbance was ended. The older sister ran around the house so overcome by the rebuke that she was more anxious to pray than to become vexed with sister, whose family name was "Baby."

His son Atticus has told me how that more than once there was not money enough on hand to mail "The Way of Life," but in answer to prayer the necessary amount would come in just in time to save the disappointment it would have caused to the many anxious ones waiting for their weekly feast. By every token, we ought to be more prompt in meeting an obligation with those who so kindly trust us.

These were days when Indian Springs Holiness Camp-ground was becoming established, and as the time was drawing near for the camp-meeting, and as a matter of course all the family wanted to attend, they did not see how it was possible, as the money was not in sight.

They had prayed over it, and had all decided to stay at home, if it was God's will, and just let papa go by himself, when he came in from town, where he had made some purchases, and began counting out his change and found three pennies, which turned out to be three five-dollar gold pieces. He had "Billie," the horse, hitched to the buggy, hurried back to the different places he had been that morning, but not a trace could be found from where the gold pieces came. So he decided that the Lord wanted them all to go to the camp-meeting, and they did.

3 d

I do not know how this impresses the reader, but the writer is simple enough to believe that if it was necessary, our God is able to make five-dollar gold pieces out of pennies, rather than deny one of His saints the greatest pleasure of his life. The writer gets much joy in believing this way about it.

I could tell many striking things in the life of this man of God, but I have said enough to convince any one that his influence was a wonderful help and encouragement to the one who was fortunate enough to be associated with him.

The best of all, this kind of a life here helps us on to a country where we will have such companionship forever and ever.

In His service,

CHARLIE D. TILLMAN.

Atlanta, Ga.

FROM ONE WHO KNEW HIM WELL.

Brother Dodge was such a patient, sweet-spirited man! Having been associated with him for eight years in the office of "The Way of Life," I never saw him in a bad humor—a fact which has made a lasting impression on me. I loved him! He was my friend. F. R. SEABORN.

Fairmont, Ga., June 8, 1906.

AS A PASTOR.

Just one short year was it my privilege to have that man of God as my pastor.

He was a wonder to me, because he was always happy in Jesus. I said, "How is this, brother?" He replied, "I am obliged to be happy, because God has given me a clean heart."

I said, "Do you believe that He would give me a clean heart?"

"Certainly, God is no respecter of persons."

He made the way so plain I grasped it at once, and in a short time after that I found Jesus, my Sanctifier. He gave me a clean heart also. Twenty-eight years have passed, and I have never ceased to praise God for the teaching I received from Brother Dodge.

The Holy Ghost was ever in him a well of water, springing up unto everlasting life. Always diligent about the Father's business.

Sabbath morning, after an early breakfast, he, with regularity, hastened to the mission Sabbath-school, where he made every one glad. From there to church, where he held an experience meeting for one hour before preaching. Sad hearts were relieved, and happy hearts rejoiced, as we talked, sang and prayed in that meeting.

His sermons always fed the flock. No one could say they went from his meetings unfed. The joy of the Lord shining out from his face was an inspiration to his hearers. In those days he was an earnest student, and to him the Bible was the "Book of all books."

He visited his people and studied their needs, hoping thereby to be a blessing to them. The desolate widow and the lonely orphan never failed to find a friend in Brother Dodge.

Being well informed on almost every subject that would concern his people, he was enabled to advise when it was needed. He always took a bold stand for God and the right, and advised his people that way regardless of consequences. God stood with him, and always brought him out on "the victory side."

At one place where he was serving, he made a fight on alcohol. The demon of the pit rose against him in such power he was at times forced to give up and lie down, but God was with him all through the mighty conflict, finally bringing him out victorious. Great rejoicing followed when the alcohol was poured on the ground. From that day to this that town has never been ruled by alcohol. That year's training established Brother Dodge and made him strong to endure the persecutions that awaited him.

From time to time, as I met him in different places, his humility deeply impressed me. He seemed to stand still, while the Lord God fought all his battles.

If we could look into heaven to-day and ask the Father His opinion of Brother Dodge as a pastor, His answer might be something like this: "I am so well pleased with him as a shepherd I would be glad to reproduce his example a million times over this earth, because My people would be fed and not scattered, as they are to-day."

I am glad that he was looking for the King before he went to heaven, because a crown of life is promised to those who "love His appearing."

Our separation from our brother will be short. The day dawn is upon us. "The coming of the Lord draweth nigh," when those who sleep in Jesus will come with him. "Blessed and holy is he that hath part in the first resurrection; on such the second death hath no power, but they shall be priests of God and of Christ, and shall reign with Him a thousand years."

Let us be glad and give honor to Him; for the marriage of the Lamb is come and His bride hath made herself ready.

MRS. SARAH D. WOOTEN.

Milledgeville, Ga., February 21, 1906.

AS EDITOR.

"Doing good of every possible sort, and as far as possible to all men, especially to them who are of the household of faith or groaning so to be."

This must have been the sentiment which glowed in the heart of W. A. Dodge, finding its expression in the undertaking of an onerous task with which he had no familiarity, that of editing and publishing a religious paper. Without newspaper training, without experience, without type or presses, and without money, he entered upon an untried field of Christian work; and for thirteen years he stuck to the task thrust upon him, believing that he was doing good and promoting the interest of the Kingdom of God among men; and amid environments that would have crushed any but an extraordinary man, he won victory for his Lord.

The painful anxiety, and mental and physical toil incident to the publication of a holiness paper in the pioneer days of that movement in Georgia, endured by Brother Dodge and his wife and children, will not be known until the secrets of all hearts are told, and God shall reward the martyrs who did not die by stake and fagot, but who, for the sake of His cause, patiently endured toil, and care, and anxiety, by the day, and by the month, and for years.

Early in the year 1882 Revs. A. J. Jarrell, George H. Patillo, W. C. Dunlap, E. G. Murrah and W. A. Dodge met together in Milledgeville, Ga., in the office of Rev. Elam Christian, and, after deliberation and much prayer, decided to begin the publication of a holiness paper in Georgia. It was also decided that W. A. Dodge should be the Editor and Elam Christian the Publisher.

On the 6th day of March, 1882, if I make no mistake, the first copy came from the press. It was called "The Tongue of Fire," but was some time afterward changed to "The Way of Life." It was a small affair—four pages, four columns to the page, and offered at fifty cents a year; but it was filled with sound doctrine and had the shine of truth on its infant face, and was destined to do a mighty work in the spiritual uplift of Georgia Methodism on the line of Scriptural holiness.

The five itinerant preachers who officiated at this birth have all gone to heaven except one, Rev. E. G. Murrah, of Macon, Ga., who yet lingers among us, one of the "Old Guards" of the North Georgia Conference, who waits the summons that will bring him to that eternal fellowship with Jarrell, Patillo, Dunlap and Dodge. What a joy of companionship will that be!

After it had been published about a year by Rev. Elam Christian, Brother Dodge borrowed some money and bought out the publisher's interest, took entire charge, and, with the help of his wife and children, ran the paper.

On the 24th day of May, 1884, "The Way of Life" was enlarged to a five column, four page paper,

PUBLISHED WEEKLY. "FIRST PURE—THEN MATURE." $1.00 PER ANNUM.

THE WAY OF LIFE.

VOL. XI. ATLANTA, GA., MARCH 8, 1893. No. 37.

"THE LIFE-BOAT."

We're floating down the stream of time,
We hav'nt got long to stay;
The stormy clouds of darkness,
Will turn to brighter day.
Then let us all take courage,
For we're not left alone,
The life-boat soon is coming
To gather the jewels home.

CHORUS:

Then cheer, my brothers, cheer,
Our trials will soon be o'er;
Our loved ones we shall meet, shall meet,
Upon the golden shore.
We're pilgrims and we're strangers here,
We're seeking a city to come,
The life-boat soon is coming
To gather the jewels home.

We sometimes feel discouraged
And think it is all in vain,
For us to live a Christian life
And walk in Jesus' name.
But then we hear the Master say,
"I'll lend you a helping hand;
And if you'll only trust me,
I'll guide you to that land."

The life-boat soon is coming,
By an eye of faith I see
As she sweeps through the water
To rescue you and me,
And land us safely in the port
With friends we love so dear.
"Get ready!" cries the captain,
Oh, look! she's almost here.

THE EVILS OF THEATRE-GOING.

"Love not the world, neither the things that are in the world. If any man love the world, the love of the Father is not in him."—I. John ii: 15.

BY REV. CLEMENT C. CARY.

One phase of the world, loved by men to their hurt, is the "pleasures of the world." These pleasures branch out in many directions, but have one deadly root. One of these "pleasures," or branches, is *the theatre*, which we use as standing for shows of all kinds.

We take the ground that *the theatre*, as at present conducted, is of the world, belongs to "the things of the world," and is run and ruled by the world—that it is hurtful to our soul's best interests. To love the theatre is to love the world, and attendance upon it is to be taken as a proof of that love.

"What can you hope to accomplish by antagonizing the theatre?" we are asked. "Can you hope to stop it?" Of course, we could not expect to do so. But this is true—the pulpit must bear testimony against popular evils, as well as open sins. It must not fail to warn when danger is near. The preacher is a watchman upon the walls of Zion to warn against danger. The pulpit must be a bulwark against all wickedness, whether hidden or clearly apparent. Some consciences will be reached and stirred by talking against and showing up the evils of the theatre. God will be pleased. The Holy Spirit will endorse it, and it will be in line with God's Word. The preacher cannot stop to consider whether or not any will heed his warnings. Can he hope to close all the saloons, shut up the brothels, and break up gambling hells? Yet he must oppose these things with might and main. Opposing them, a sentiment will be created against them, and many will be saved from these snares. And so it is with the theatre.

Should the theatre be patronized? Is it right to attend such places of amusement?

The question goes beyond "Church rules," for there can be no question that it is contrary at least to Methodist rules. Besides, if it be wrong only because the Church forbids attendance upon theatres, then the further question might arise, what right has the Church to establish standards of right and wrong actions, and to forbid what is not forbidden by the Scriptures and by the spirit of religion?

Even on the ground that it is contrary to Church rules to attend the theatre, a strong argument can be framed against it. It should be sufficient to know the Church to which we belong forbids theatre-going, and we have voluntarily promised to renounce it and all other worldly things. When the Church forbids engaging in anything questionable, the presumption is that the Church is right, and honest Christian people will stop and consider before breaking over all limits. As between the individual judgment of a carnally-minded professor, who "minds the things of the flesh," and the judgment of the wisest and best men of the Church expressed in laws and rules of conduct, it will not take a moment to decide which is most likely to be right.

It ought to be a sufficient and satisfactory answer to one who has any conscience upon this question, and who honestly seeks light, to say that the theatre is of the world, belongs to the world, and is run by the world, and hence we are not to be conformed to the world nor to love the things of the world. But this is not sufficient for many who have no eyes to see "the world" in "the theatre," nor to perceive the exceeding sinfulness of worldliness.

1. The theatre is opposed by the very spirit of the Scriptures. Note such passages as these which teach the nature of true religion, show its opposition to a worldly life, and urges non-conformity to the world.

"Demas hath forsaken me, having loved this present world," and so it *may* be said of the theatre goers, that they have forsaken God because of the love of the world.

"Be not conformed to the world," says Paul. "Ye are not of the world, but I have chosen you out of the world," says Christ.

"Ye adulterers and adulteresses, know ye not that the friendship of the world is enmity with God? Whosoever therefore, will be a friend of the world is the enemy of God." James—iv: 4.

"Wherefore, come out from among them, and be *ye* separate, saith the Lord, and touch not the unclean thing."—II. Cor. vi: 17.

Study these Scriptures; for if they teach anything at all, they declare without question that Christ's people are not of the world, are not conformed to the world, are chosen out of the world and are to be separate from it, which worldliness is found in the theatre, if found anywhere, and cannot be indulged in without violating these Scriptures.

"Abstain from all appearance of evil."—I. Thes. v: 22. If the theatre has not the appearance of evil, then do all signs fail.

"Dearly beloved, abstain from fleshly lusts, which war against the soul."—I. Peter ii: 11. And in the theatre is one of those very lusts against which we are warned, for John in enumerating them in his first epistle speaks of "the lust of the eye," which finds its gratification in the sights in the play house. This is of the world and not of God, and belongs to "the flesh," which Paul talks so much about in Romans.

"Ye cannot serve God and Mammon," says Jesus; and yet, this is just what that large class of theater-going Church members are trying unsuccessfully to do.

"Ye are a holy nation, a peculiar people."—I. Peter ii: 9. Where is our peculiarity and wherein is our holiness if we are to follow after the world in its hunt after carnal pleasures? Where is separation from the world to begin if not at this point? The very lust for the theatre shows an utter lack of "that holiness, without which no man shall see the Lord."

"Lovers of pleasures more than lovers of God," is the short and pointed description given by Timothy of that worldly class who have "a form of godliness, but deny the power thereof." And among these are theatre-goers.

"If any man will come after me, let him deny himself, and come after me," are Christ's words. Where is self-denial to show itself if not at the very point we are on? For Paul writing to Titus, states that this self-denial is the very lesson of salvation: "Teaching us, that denying ungodliness and worldly lusts, (or pleasures) we should live soberly, righteously and godly in this present world."

But why quote further passages? The whole tenor of the Scriptures is against this worldly evil, clearly recognized by all religious Bible students and spiritually-minded people.

2. The example of Jesus Christ gives no encouragement to theatre-goers. He says, "Follow me." But wherein are we to follow Him? In His life, and His spirit. If He were living with us, would He frequent the modern theatre, on the wild hunt for frolic and pleasure, hungry for fun and pastime? Would He go to such a place to find instruction and to learn lessons in morals? Suppose He should visit your cities, and the theatres were in full blast, as they now are—does any one who knows anything of His life and character as revealed in the New Testament, suppose, for one moment, His face would be turned toward the play-house? His feet might lead Him up in that section of the city, but He would more than likely be found preaching on the streets to dying men as they passed by. Or He would seek some house of prayer, as His custom was when on earth. If some noted actor were to play one of Shakespeare's plays—and He were honored with a complimentary ticket—even this would not allure or tempt Him to go to such pleasure halls. He might attend if He were allowed to go on the stage; not as an actor, but to speak to immortal beings about their souls. If Jesus would not attend such places as a pleasure seeker, (and remember He was a young man) you, as a follower of Him, cannot afford to attend such resorts of pleasure. Where is it recorded that He sought out and attended places for pleasure? He had neither time nor inclination for such things.

As Jesus Christ is given as a practical example to be followed, so God has given but one standard for living, to both preachers and laymen. Is it right for Church members to attend theatres? Then it is not wrong for their preacher to go. Is it not right for your pastor to patronize such resorts of pleasure, where the world is found assembled in force? Then is it not right for the pastor's members to patronize it. It is no more harm for one than the other.

Yet how unreasonable and inconsistent do some people talk! Not one of them but will tell you the theatre is not a proper place for a minister of the Gospel. They know his influence will be lost and his piety will be seriously injured. Yet, with the same law for preachers and laymen, they cry out, "no harm to go to the theatre." What preacher ever attended a theatre without being seriously hurt in his influence over men? These same theatre-going people would not wish to have a theatre-going preacher at their bedside when dying to minister to and pray for them. They want a holy man for such offices.

3. *The theatre is irreligious* and anti-religious in its make-up. Not only is there nothing in it that is religious; in many of its phases, it is positively opposed to the religion of the Bible. Its spirit is contrary to the very spirit of Christianity, and an enemy to all vital godliness. The very atmosphere of the place is death to everything spiritual. All its surroundings and accompaniments lead the mind away from God. They tend to forgetfulness of the brevity of life and the solemnities of eternity, and beget and favor a spirit that is carnal, worldly and ungodly. There is nothing in or belonging to it favorable to Scriptural piety. Here the world is massed in force, and Jesus Christ and His claims are neither known nor recognized. A decidedly worldly spirit pervades the whole place and governs the people found there.

The name of God is not unfrequently taken in vain publicly by unhallowed lips on the stage; prayer is often made a solemn mockery; religion is ridiculed, vice is robbed of its most hideous features, and sin is made attractive and pleasing.

The very plays are often wicked and anti-religious, bringing to the front the wicked and illustrating the vile among men and women. Lest the statement be charged as overdrawn or untrue, let me give some testimony from the stage itself.

Lillie Lewis, a noted actress, is recently reported in a daily paper as giving utterance to the following:

"Some folks condemn actresses for playing bad women. What are they to play, then? Surely not good, easy, common-place, every day women in whose uneventful lives there is nothing dramatic—no flashing up of the darker passions. Who would go to the theatre to see a star interpret the life of a Sunday-school teacher or a sister of charity?"

This is pretty good evidence upon the point, and proves just what we have declared, but just what many of the defenders of the play-house have no eyes to see. Of course they "interpret bad women," for plays of a more moral character would not bring the crowds; and money is what the theatre wants, even though the morals are corrupted.

During my pastorate in a town in Georgia, twice within a short time, shows were advertised to take place in an opera house owned by a Methodist official, proposing to bring religion into ridicule. The fences contained show bills at one time advertising the "Deacon's Dance," the very name of which contained a lie. It was a hit at Church officials, the tendency of which was to make light of Church officers and popularize the dance.

At another time, a show visited the town which advertised a caricature of the "Salvation Army," with "come and be shaved," and "a new salvation." I protested to the owner of the opera house against it in the name of my Master, and this feature, so objectionable, was promised to be omitted. Yet so-called Christian people were ready to patronize and encourage it.

This very same show, from all reports, was so disgusting and offensive to even theatre-goers (who can stand almost anything) that some of them could not stomach it. Even the town paper spoke disparagingly of it. Quite a wonder! for when the average secular paper cannot stand a company or a play, there must be something awful in it.

And such shows come along semi-occasionally heralded by bills posted on your buildings and fences, advertising scenes which are a scandal, a reflection on the Christian sentiment of the community, and the tendency of which is to bring religion into disrepute.

The "plays" are not selected with a view to convey moral truth and to teach virtue, but of at the expense of virtue and the loss of morality. Everything is sacrificed in order to get money; and so in order to make a popular hit and successful run, the baser and coarser feelings are appealed to. No matter what the play is the great end is money receipts.

Moral and instructive plays would bankrupt any theatrical company very quickly, because of the depraved and vitiated tastes of the people. This sort will not be supported. Think of this, when you hear people talk of the valuable truths learned at the theatre.

We are told, "valuable lessons in virtue and morality are there taught." Who goes to the theatre to be instructed? Not one in forty. The great bulk of people go there to be amused. They are hunting fun and amusement. This is their aim and desire. When people wish to learn lessons in virtue and morals, they go elsewhere than the average theatre.

All this talk about the theatre being instructive is pure imagination—a mere pretext and a snare, to bolster up this school of evil. Some of you have attended theatres. Tell me candidly, what lessons of virtue, morality or religion have you learned at the expense of money wasted and time thrown away? What vices have been so portrayed as to lead you to hate and turn from them? Wherein have you been made better as a citizen, a husband, or a wife, a son or a daughter? Has it made you more benevolent, kind-hearted, virtuous, sober, truthful and Christ-like? Where are those addicted to strong drink, who have been reformed through this great so-called moral agency? Where are those who have become more liberal and God-fearing? Who has been led away from an abandoned and lecherous life? Where are they who have graduated in this great school of morals and virtue? It would be refreshing to see those people who have been educated on a better line of morals. On the other hand, see how many have been led into bad company, late hours, wasteful habits, and even to worse places and into more serious evils. Here the ground has been laid for departure from God, and the first steps taken in a wicked and worldly career. Even as this is written, news comes of a young bank cashier gone wrong for a large amount, a fugitive from justice, who was noted for his extravagance, his club life, and his high and costly boxes at the theatre—the latter in close companionship with other evils, and having to do with them. Instead of being a school of virtue, it has practically been a school of vice, more especially to the young. Virtue has been often made to appear hideous and vice attractive. The latter has often been so clothed and lionized as to be attractive, while virtue has been so caricatured as to be put below par.

An afternoon paper of a certain Georgia city heads an editorial with "A Sermon on the Stage," from which I beg leave to dissent:

"If the clergymen of Augusta had been in the theatre last night they would have heard and seen a sermon on the stage better than most of them have preached in many a long day. A lesson in real life, every day life, with 'Men and Women' as the subject and the actors, was taught to the people, and the impression made was deeper and more lasting than is made in a large majority of the pulpits of the country. Men and women were shown how easy it is to sin, to take the first wrong step in speculation and shady transactions in business, and how a single impulsive act grows into breach of trust and a big defalcation. They were shown how hard it is to confess and correct such an overt act, and how the punishment of such a sin is only ended among men in the grave."

If this be correct, then verily many very poor sermons must have been delivered in pulpits. But who believes this but the editor himself? Verily, this is a new thing under the sun. Better inaugurate a theatrical pulpit, and preach to dying men the new Gospel which theatres teach. The whole thing is so ridiculous that it is surprising to read it. And yet this is the sort of defense which is made of the theatre. Not satisfied with putting the stage on a par with the pulpit; here it is placed above the pulpit in the character of its teachings and in its impressions on human hearts. Who believes it?

If it be a school of virtue, who are its teachers? Who are these instructors in morals? If sermons are preached, who are the preachers? What is their moral character? Will you sit at the feet of a rake, an adulterer, a licentious man, to learn lessons of chastity and moral purity? Will you have your wife and young daughter learn lessons in lady-like modesty, from her, who is bold and brazen enough to appear in public in tights, or with scarcity of apparel, and thus wantonly expose her person to public gaze without a blush? Will you have them taught lessons of womanly devotion and instructed in the duties of wives and mothers by her, who has been untrue to her marriage vows, or who has been separated or divorced from her husband? Will your refined, modest and virtuous wives and girls have as their tutors in public those between whom and the purest and best society, an impassable line is drawn? Will a profane man teach you reverence, or an intemperate man instruct you in sobriety? Will any good lessons be taught by Sabbath-breaking, ungodly, and profane actors, who fear not God, nor keep His commandments? Will you matriculate your boy in such a school, or send your girl to be taught by such teachers? Yet are you asked to do this very thing, (and some do it) with the plea that moral lessons are taught at the theatre!

Even if the "plays" contained good lessons, the surroundings are so unfavorable for the pupils, that any good impressions are soon lost upon those who witness them. The amount of good taught and received in theatres is like a grain of wheat in a cart load of chaff—like a seed of barley in a yard full of cockleburs—like a single blade of grass among a yard full of weeds and briars—like reaching for a grain of gold down in a barrel of sewerage.

[CONCLUDED IN NEXT ISSUE.]

COPY OF "THE WAY OF LIFE,"
Published for years by Rev. W. A. Dodge, in the interest of the Scriptural Doctrine of Holiness.

nearly double its former size, and the price advanced to one dollar a year.

During his incumbency of the editor's chair Brother Dodge served the following appointments: Eatonton Station, Grace Church, Atlanta (which he built) ; Gainesville, Cartersville, Bolton circuit, Fulton circuit, Forsyth circuit, Walker Street, Atlanta and Southside Mission, Atlanta. Three years he was supernumerary, on account of throat trouble.

Some idea of the work done by the paper, and its circulation, may be inferred from the fact that when it left his hands there was due Brother Dodge on his books as much as $6,000.

In 1895, Brother Dodge consented to the merging of "The Way of Life" into "The Methodist," edited by Rev. H. C. Morrison and published at Louisville, Ky., to whom the paper was sold. To show the mind of Brother Dodge, we quote from his words in the last editorial he wrote for the paper:

"We never started out to be the Editor and Publisher of a paper, but it was thrust upon us in such a way that we could not say no. All along we have been ready to turn it over when we felt convinced that it would be for the glory of God in the advancement of the Holiness Movement."

Editor Morrison wrote when the papers were united:

" 'The Way of Life' was the Morning Star paper in the Holiness Movement in the South. It has done a noble work. Only eternity can tell the thousands of souls that have been led on to full salvation by the instructions contained in its columns. It has always been true as the needle to the pole, and sweet in spirit as the honey of Canaan. May God's blessing rest upon Brother Dodge's work and his devoted family, who so faithfully stood by him in his battle for the greatest doctrine of Methodism."

W. O. BUTLER,

North Georgia Conference.

Chickamauga, Ga.

NORTH GEORGIA HOLINESS CONVENTION.

The following notice of the spring meeting of this Convention will bring up sweet memories to some who have lived in the past. It is taken from an old copy of "The Way of Life," of March 8, 1893. Interest attaches to it, because Brother Dodge was the leading spirit in the meeting:

"The Spring Meeting of the North Georgia Holiness will be held with the Hamilton Street Church, Dalton, Ga., April 24-30, Rev. M. B. Smith, pastor. Begin at once to arrange for going. But do not forget to fast and pray for a wonderful baptism of the Holy Ghost. We must, under God, have many souls saved and sanctified at this meeting.

"All are invited to come, whether they are in the experience or not. We expect to have Rev. George D. Watson with us, D. V., and also others."

AS ONE OF THE FOUNDERS OF THE IN-DIAN SPRING CAMP-MEETING.

While not the first of the preachers of the Georgia Conferences to come into the knowledge and experience of entire sanctification, which, according to Dr. Lovick Pierce, had "been lost from the church," Brother Dodge, from his first entering into the experience, became one of the leaders of the movement. He soon became almost its embodiment. It is safe to say that no ten men did as much to forward the cause.

"The Way of Life," which he for so many years published alone and on his own responsibility, so carried the elementary teachings of the experience into Methodist circles, and so demonstrated its claims as a Methodist and Scriptural doctrine, that to-day the suspension, or merging, of that paper is a regret to hundreds yet living.

The writer well remembers once, when shaken in his own steadfastness, and pressed to a choice between compromise and Conference unpopularity, as the devil pictured it, a sentence in a letter from Brother Dodge lighted up the way and strengthened him to walk in it: "From the first I had to be definite, and God has made it a great blessing to me."

We will never forget his big, happy face at our own Conference, where, although knowing that he was preaching a doctrine unpopular with most of the preachers, and feared by many, he was, in the sweetness of perfect love, pressing what he knew to be his church's doctrine, and, his church's hope.

When the paper changed form and hands, and our brother went back to his full Conference work with all his time and powers, his zeal for the "central idea of Christianity" still burned beyond the possibility of confinement. His association with the movement in other places prepared him to see the importance of propagating the truth in the old Methodist way of a great central camp-meeting. It was in his heart that the work, so widely known from the Indian Spring center, was projected. The "largest and best appointed camp-meeting in the South" was seen by faith and love, before others had thought of it at all.

It was during the South Georgia Holiness meeting in Waycross, in the fall of 1889, that the matter was first mentioned. It found a responsive chord, and with a profound sense that an important movement was about to be projected, the friends present waited for the unfolding of the plans, and the suggestion of the fittest place for locating the camp-ground. All instinctively depended upon the one man, who had so proven his capacity and devotion, that we felt, difficult as the new movement was, love would find the way and God would assist.

In God's providence, the spring meeting of the Association was held in a little saw-mill town called Ashburn, now the county-seat of Turner county. We wondered, as we looked out on the town the morning after our arrival, why we had been directed to so small and unpromising a field.

Brother Dodge, as usual, was present, leading the services.

It was this meeting that proved to be God's plan for making possible the project of the camp-meeting. Lumber and building assistance from friends, who saw the great light during this week of fruitful service, were contributions as large as they were timely. It was one of the providential links in carrying forward that which had been begun with faith in God to further His plans. It was a common thing to stop in the midst of any work we might be doing together on the camp-ground and engage in prayer. When we walked over the ground near the spring, seeking out a location for the establishing of this sacred place, he proposed that we kneel there in the depth of the woods and ask Divine guidance.

He always said that he thought the Lord was in the choice which was made.

The site had been selected during the Christmas week following the fall meet in Waycross in 1889. Brother Dodge, accompanied by H. A. Hodges, J. H. Curry and the writer, walked that memorable day over much of the ground from Flovilla to Indian Spring, seeking the location.

More than once during the day the quartette kneeled and sought direction as to the best place, and when it was thought that the proper site had been found, we prayed again that God would overrule and change the choice if He saw best. This He did in a way to show that He had heard the prayer, and the present location proved manifestly better in every way, and was finally chosen.

Well does the writer remember the Tuesday morning before the appointed first meeting, when, having boarded the train in Waycross Monday night, he arrived on the camp-ground a little after sun-up on Tuesday, and saw Brothers Dodge and Hodges, dressed in overalls, and with mattock and hoe, diligently clearing the undergrowth in the grove of thick oaks leading to the ten acres which then composed the grounds.

The two had been a week on the grounds cleaning up and putting up some small tents, which had been given Brother Dodge by the Illinois Holiness Association, and also erecting a large cloth tent, loaned for the occasion, and under which the first meeting on the ground was held.

It is needless to say that no man put more earnest and hard work on the ground than did Brother Dodge. Ably assisted by Brother Hodges, of like practical ability, he was everywhere to be seen, and no work was too hard, or too soiling to hands or overalls, for him to perform it.

And this was true to the last. Always busy with fresh details and improvements, for a day or two after the meeting began it was a marvel to some of us how he could still be so fully into every service. It was truly the "joy of the Lord" that sustained and refreshed him.

We will never forget the day when the new improvements were finished, and he had come regularly into the worship under the tabernacle. It seemed that the Lord especially rewarded him for his faithfulness. The mighty tide of the Spirit's inflowing seemed to be almost more than he could bear. The beaming face and dilating form were a picture never to be forgotten. The writer called his own little son to his side and said: "Take that scene well into your mind. You will not see his like again in this world. It is a picture of God rewarding His faithful servant, and it is a foretaste of heaven."

We still cherish that picture on that occasion in that place as a rich reminder of the last and Great Holiness Meeting where we confidently expect, through the keeping grace of God, to meet him again!

It was perhaps three years before his death, that sitting one moonlight night after a hard day's work of preparation for the next camp-meeting, and speaking of his love for the beautiful and hallowed grounds, that he said, "I would like to be buried here where heaven has always seemed so near, and where God is working so mightily to quicken His church and by that means to save the world."

He felt, as others of us feel, that there is no spot on earth where it would be more easy and natural to meet and greet the Lord than here, where He has always seemed so near, and has so revealed His glory.

Dublin, Ga.   G. W. MATHEWS,
                         South Georgia Conference.

RECOLLECTIONS BY MRS. W. A. DODGE.

In 1869 we were married. That year Mr. Dodge was instrumental in building Evans' Chapel, Atlanta, now Walker Street Church. In 1871 we were sent to Dahlonega, the charge composed of one Church in town and three in the country. One was at Gaddistown, sixteen miles distant. The former pastor had used a borrowed horse for his country appointments, but now there was no horse in town, either to hire or borrow. Mr. Dodge, however, managed, in January and February, to secure an animal, but in March he failed. When the day came to leave for Gaddistown he went up town to see if he could secure a way to get to his appointment, but met with failure. When he came back I told him not to go—that there would only be a few out to hear him anyway. His reply was, "Yes, that is so, but I must go." This was his life-long rule—to go to the post of duty at any cost. When I asked him how he was going, he quickly replied he would walk. And walk he did. He left me, starting out to go sixteen miles across the Blue Ridge Mountains, a very rough and steep way to travel. He reached Gaddistown about sundown, preached that night and the next day at 11 o'clock. Then, starting back home, he preached at another appointment at 3 p.m., and again at night. Coming to Jones's Chapel, three miles from home, he preached the next Sunday at 11 o'clock, when a good brother was thoughtful enough to go out and bring him home.

His feet were so blistered and he was so sore, he could scarcely walk for several days. After he had left home on this trip mentioned, several called at the house to see him, when I told them he had gone over the mountains to his appointment. "How did he go, Sister Dodge?" was asked. "He walked," I replied. And I cried myself sick about it.

But there was a happy sequel to it. The people were exceedingly sorry when they heard of his walking to his appointment, and said it should never occur again. So Monday afternoon Brother William Worley came riding up to the parsonage with a beautiful horse and saddle, and said: "Brother Dodge, this is your horse. The citizens, after they found that you had been compelled to walk to your churches, made up a purse, and bought this horse for you." No more blistered feet now!

When Conference removed us from Dahlonega he left seven preaching places for the poor people in that section. Then Mr. Dodge was on the Dahlonega District two years, and on the Gainesville District one year. From there we went to St. Paul's, Atlanta, where he finished paying for the church building and erected a parsonage. From there we went to Sparta, staying two years. He soon discovered there was no preaching at the cotton factory nearby, and organized a Sunday-school, where he went every Sunday morning at 8 o'clock, then back

4 d

to town to preaching, the town Sunday-school being in the afternoon. Every Tuesday night he preached to the factory people, for he always had a tender feeling for these hard-working people.

I remember that year Bishop Pierce's granddaughter married at the church, and Rev. Lovick Pierce performed the ceremony. We were invited to the church, and also to the reception. But it was Tuesday night, the occasion of preaching to the factory people, so we went to the factory, then back to the reception. Of course, we were late. Bishop Pierce met us at the door and said, very pleasantly, "Very fashionable pastor and wife!" Mr. Dodge said, "Bishop, I went to fill my appointment at the factory first." The bishop replied, "God bless you, Brother Dodge! Duty before pleasure with you always." How true was that of him!

After leaving Sparta we were sent to Eatonton, living there four years. Here we found a nice town, but there were seven bar-rooms in it. Mr. Dodge commenced immediately in dead earnest to work for their overthrow. Every week he prepared an article for the town paper on temperance, and on acount of his great activity on this burning question many hard things were said about him. But he was not turned aside. He kept on working and praying, and the second year all the bar-rooms were put out of business except one.

While he was at Conference at the close of his second year, some one in Eatonton was expressing publicly a wish for him to be sent back again. An old darkey, hearing the remark, said, "I don't know what you want Mr. Dodge to come back for. He has got all the bar-rooms out but one, and if he comes back again, he will get that one clean out, too." He came back, and the darkey was right—the last bar-room did get out.

That year we had a wonderful meeting, the best I ever saw. Everybody seemed to get religion, and the liquor had to go. Mr. Dodge was the happiest man I ever saw. He would walk the streets nearly all day long, and rejoice, "The victory! The victory! God has given us the victory!"

The brethren gave him a well-filled purse and a vacation after this, in order to go off and rest. But instead of doing so he went to Cartersville, Ga., and helped the pastor, Rev. A. J. Jarrell, ten days. He would not take time to rest—said he "would rather wear out than rust out."

He was put on the Atlanta City Mission in 1883, when he succeeded in building what was then Grace Church, now a strong city charge, erecting a fine building. They were enabled to worship in the basement April 20, 1884. He preached his first sermon in it on "Gratitude and Courage."*

In 1885, he went to Gainesville; in 1886, to Cartersville, then to Fulton Circuit, just outside of Atlanta. During the years 1895, 1896 and 1897, he took a supernumerary relation, living in Atlanta. He

---

*NOTE —It is a coincidence that just about the time Sister Dodge was writing the article above in which she refers to the erection of Grace Church, Atlanta, under her husband's ministry, this same church had erected and was preparing to dedicate a handsome edifice, costing many thousand dollars, to take the place of the first building.

helped very much Brother Thomas C. Mayson in his
mission work on Peters Street, a locality noted for
its great sinfulness in this large city. Here a Sunday-school was in operation, prayer-meeting held
every Sunday morning at 8 o'clock, and a breakfast
served for the poor people at 9 o'clock. The first
Thanksgiving dinner these people ever saw was arranged by Mr. Dodge (see newspaper clipping below) and Brother Mayson.

The last charge he served before he left us for
heaven was St. James', Atlanta, where he received
over one hundred members.

So it will be found he was a Sunday-school worker, temperance laborer, a faithful preacher, a toiler
on missions, one who did his best in every place in
which he found himself in the providence of God.
Blessed man!

East Point, Ga.   Mrs. W. A. Dodge.

After Sister Dodge wrote the foregoing, and in
close connection with Brother Dodge's work as Atlanta City Missionary, and the starting of what is
now Grace church, one of the leading Methodist
congregations in Atlanta, the following card was
found among his "sketches" of sermons, which gives
an item of interest about the erection of the first
Methodist structure in that part of the city, which
marked the beginning of that influential church. It
is an appeal for help:

"Atlanta, Ga., May 1, 1883.

"The City Missionary has much expense unprovided for, such as rents, lights, Sunday-school literature, and many calls from the poor, etc.

"He is now trying to build a plank tabernacle on Houston street, between Jackson and Boulevard, where he can begin to preach and hold Sunday-school, prayer-meetings, etc. Brother Brewer, a member of First church, has been employed for a month, at least, to help in visiting, and securing money and subscriptions for the new church on the Boulevard.

"Will you help him? Anything, much or little. Please put the amount on this card, and drop in the collection-basket to-day.

"The money you can hand to the pastor, the City Missionary, or to Brother Brewer.

"W. A. DODGE,
"Atlanta City Missionary."

"I promise to pay the sum of $........ for the support of Atlanta City Missions during the present year, payable in installments, as follows: ....
....
Signature ....
No. ....Street."

On the back of this card is a "sketch" of a sermon, when and where preached is not stated, possibly while he was working at that point.

Text.—Numbers 10: 29: "And Moses said unto

Hobab, We are journeying unto the place of which
the Lord said, I will give it to you! come thou with
us, and we will do thee good, for the Lord hath
spoken good concerning Israel."

I. Israel was journeying—
    1. They were in Egypt.
    2. They were on their way to Canaan.

II. They were unselfish—
    1. They wanted others to go with them.
    2. They were willing to divide.
    3. They could safely promise them good—
       "for the Lord hath spoken good concerning
       Israel."
       a. He was able to perform.
       b. He did perform.
       c. And they did divide.

FROM AN OLD COPY OF "THE WAY OF LIFE."

The Cordele District Holiness Meeting will be
held at Ty-Ty, Georgia. Those going will please
send their names to Rev. J. J. Williams, Ty-Ty, at
once, that homes may be provided.

Revs. R. O. Smith and D. M. Crawford will be
present to help the home force push the battle. The
time will be March 20.

Ashburn, Ga.   J. LAWRENCE.

HOW THE POOR WERE FED AT THE GOSPEL MISSION.

The following account of this interesting incident,
referred to in the foregoing article by Mrs. W. A.
Dodge, is taken from an Atlanta, Ga., paper, which
appeared the next day:

"Thanksgiving day was more than a name to
about one hundred and fifty people who gathered at
the Peters Street Gospel Mission this afternoon between the hours of 12 and 2 o'clock. There a
Thanksgiving dinner was served to the poor people
of the neighborhood, and later this afternoon sundry
well-filled baskets will go out from the mission into
the homes of the sick and suffering poor in the
squalid alleys in that section of the city.

All the morning religious services were conducted
at the mission by different ministers and laymen, and
a large crowd was present. The lame, the halt and
the blind were there, for in addition to their spiritual
wants their bodily wants were supplied, and thus they
looked with much more favor on the gospel truths
that were presented to them in such a substantial
manner.

A HUNDRED WERE FED.

"Mr. T. C. Mayson, the founder of the mission,
Rev. W. A. Dodge, and others, wore beaming faces
when the hour for serving the dinner arrived. There
were in the rooms of the mission about a hundred

people, some of them wan-faced children who had
never known what it was to have a good square meal.
They had heard of Thanksgiving dinners, but regarded them as something afar off, in some enchant-
ed land, to which they never expected to draw near.
When they stood face to face with a genuine Thanksgiving dinner, with turkey and trimmings, their
pleasure can better be imagined than described.

"As the hour of noon approached the children
had their eyes fixed on the back door, for just outside, behind the mission, the dinner was being prepared. A long counter stood there over which was
an awning to shut off the dampness of the morning.

"On this counter was a pile of good things—turkeys, chickens, roast beef, roast mutton, cake, pies,
sweet fresh rolls, crackers, celery, cranberry sauce,
and everything else that could go to make a good dinner.

"A number of ladies and gentlemen, with sleeves
rolled up, were at work carving up the meats and
serving the plates that were piled up around them.
Each plate was filled until it could hold no more, and
when all were ready the door was opened and the
workers at the mission, both old and young, carried
the plates in and passed them out until everybody
was supplied.

"It would have done the heart of any man good
to have seen the looks of gratitude that settled on
the face of one poor woman and her six children, all
little fellows, as they saw the tempting food. They
are very poor and the only square meals they ever

get are at the mission where they go regularly every Sunday morning. To-day the meal was square with an extra crown of good things on top to run it over.

HAD NEVER SEEN TURKEY.

"The children didn't know what the turkey was, and had to be told. Their delight knew no bounds when they realized that they were actually eating sure enough turkey and cranberry sauce. Some old men were there and old women, and their eyes, dimmed with age, were streaming as they took with thankful hearts the food that was given them, suggesting to some better days they had known in the long ago when they lived in comfort on the old plantation where want never showed his haggard face.

"The dinner was served from 12 to 2, and somewhere in the neighborhood of 200 people were fed. This afternoon when order has been fully restored all the food that is left will be taken out to the highways and hedges to feed those who were unable to come to the dinner. In many of the lanes and alleys running off from Peters street there are bedridden poor, some paralyzed and others dying for the delicacies of life. The good men and women of the mission have hunted them out, and since the place has been opened these poor have been fed. To-day they were made unusually glad by the abundance of good things that were brought them.

"Among the articles of food sent in to the mission this morning were seven fine turkeys, a large number of chickens, 200 light rolls, an endless quantity of light bread, several big boxes filled with roast beef and roast mutton, three boxes of cakes, genuine cake with icing on the top, and then there were biscuits, sweetmeats and crackers.

"To make the day one of genuine thanks a box of hats, twelve in number, and a quite as large quantity of clothing for all classes, were sent out and distributed among the poor. It was a day of genuine thanksgiving, and long will it be remembered by the workers and attendants at the mission."

A LETTER FROM BISHOP J. S. KEY.

Sherman, Texas, February 1, 1904.

MY DEAR SISTER DODGE: I give you my sympathy and prayers in this the darkest hour of your life. You are sorely bereaved, and so am I. The best friend of my whole life is gone. I counseled with him and confided in him, and loved him. He was worthy of it, and I knew it.

I have known him from his boyhood, and never saw in him one solitary wrong act or suspected in him a wrong motive. He was the Lord's own, and is at home with the God he loved and served.

I mourn for you and for myself. The loss is ours. The gain is his. I am trying to live so as to meet him. The thought of it relieves the sorrow over his loss.

God bless you, my afflicted sister, and give you support in this dark hour.

Affectionately,

(Signed)   JOSEPH S. KEY.

CONVERTED UNDER HIS MINISTRY.

When I was quite a boy Rev. W. A. Dodge was a young preacher, and held a protracted meeting at old Mt. Charlotte schoolhouse in the summer of 1866. I was fourteen years old, and was going to school. The teacher would let us out for the eleven o'clock service. After one week, all of the ministerial help left him. Monday morning came, and Brother Dodge, in his jovial way, said, "I am all alone to-day, but I will do my best to pull the load." He held the meeting under a bush arbor at the back of the schoolhouse, as the house was crowded.

After one of the best sermons I ever heard, from Romans 8: 14: "For as many as are led by the Spirit of God, they are the sons of God," I made a surrender to God, and when I left my seat to give my hand to join the church, God wonderfully saved my soul before I got to the preacher, who took me in his arms and shouted for joy. Oh, what a bright spot in my history!

After a short time he lost his wife, and in the course of time married my aunt, Mary Jones, which made the tie between us all the stronger.

After several years he sold out his paper, "The Way of Life," and went out in the evangelistic work. So we traveled together a good deal. In the summer of 1897 we went to Monticello, Ga., to hold a three-weeks' meeting in the Methodist church. Rev. H. L. Embry was the pastor, and we had a hard pull

the first week. The second week it got better, and
the people got to confessing and making up with
their neighbors, and getting their accounts straight-
ened up with each other. The third week the hoops
fell down and the staves fell in, and there was a
glorious time in the old town of Monticello.

The last night of the meeting the devil overdid his
work in sending a one-legged, drunken man to the
church. While the preaching was going on, the poor
man fell asleep, and a bottle of whiskey fell out of his
pocket and broke and spilled out on the floor, and
later a pistol fell out. When the meeting closed his
friends began to beg for him. The pastor was firm
and was going to present him to the grand jury.
Before we left Monday morning his wife came in,
begging the pastor for him, and before we left
Brother Dodge's great big heart, which was always
full of love for poor dying men, got to begging the
pastor for him, too, and under some good promises
from the poor sinner, the pastor pushed the case no
further.

We traveled together, talked together, prayed together, slept together. He preached and I tried to
sing, while we worked for God, trying to get people
saved.

In 1899 we went to Indian Spring Camp-meeting.
One night, after the lights were all out and the good
people had retired, some mischievous boys went to
the tabernacle to hold a mock service. Hearing them
from the preacher's tent, Brother Dodge arose, and
several followed. Surrounding the tabernacle we

struck matches, and of all the running, those boys did some of it. Later he caught a young man who had violated the law on the grounds, and the begging process began again. Brother Dodge played firm. After awhile an old-maid aunt of the young culprit came to the preacher saying, "If you will let him go this time, I will get religion." Of course he was released, all of which shows this man of God could be firm to protect his Master's cause, but if you repented, the preacher would too, and the poor sinner went free.

In the spring of 1904, he left us and went up to glory; it seemed to me, still a young man. But God knew best, and does all things well. Some day we shall sing and praise God together again.

J. L. SIMS.

Hapeville, Ga., June 1, 1906.

A NOTE FROM THE FIELD.

(Found in a copy of Way of Life, March 15, 1893.)

Rev. Thomas H. Leitch, Laurens, S. C., writes: "Closed here last night an old-time meeting. The first one to get blessed was the pastor, who came out clearly into the blessing of sanctification. One Presbyterian sister found out the best she could do was to send up in smoke some thirty-six novels, and the Lord blessed her there. Somebody over here is getting mad."

WHAT I REMEMBER ABOUT REV. W. A. DODGE.

The first recollection of my friend and esteemed brother dates back to about the time when I first joined St. James Church, Augusta. His excellent mother, Mrs. Isabella Dodge, was then a member of that Church, and to know her, one will not wonder that she had such a son as Asbury Dodge.

Really, when we begin to give credit for what our good brother was, his mother, who gave him life, and from whom he received his first impressions, must not be left out of the account. To her great credit is due. Sober-minded, regular in attendance at the house of God, a woman who loved her Lord—this•was the mother of Brother Dodge.

The year after I entered upon a religious life, it became my duty to collect monthly from the members their contributions for the pastor. Regularly as the time came round, about the first of the month, she paid cheerfully, without complaint, what was assessed her, never complaining, never putting off the collector, always making it pleasant.

There comes to me now the first time I ever heard Brother Dodge preach. It was in St. James' Church. I suppose he was on a visit to his mother. His sermon was on blind Bartimeus, and while none of his points now come to mind, the subject sticks to my memory. One thing I distinctly recollect. He sang at the close, largely by himself, the song, now old, then new, "Lord Jesus, I long to be perfectly whole," and while some would now put it into the mouths of penitents seeking pardon as expressing their desires, his after-experience shows conclusively the sense in which Brother Dodge used it on that occasion.

Another recollection of him was about 1871, at a District Conference, at Sparta, Ga. Then these annual gatherings were not mere business meetings, nor cold, dull sessions, but peculiarly religious occasions, as they were originally intended to be. It was customary to have a Sunday-school anniversary on Sunday afternoon, for the District Conference always lapped over and included Sunday, many of the delegates remaining.

This anniversary was really a large children's meeting. Brother Dodge had charge of it (for he was peculiarly fitted for just such a task), and spoke, closing it with some proposition. The Lord was there, and impressions of that service remain with me till this day. Our brother, by the way, loved dearly to hold children's services, and would have made one of the finest Sunday-school agents.

A kind friend volunteers the pleasing information that every second Sunday was "Children's Day" on stations served by him, and every three months on circuits. The sermons on these occasions were addressed especially to the children, and every effort was made to bring them to Christ. In fact, he was an all-round man, fitting most any place in which you could put him, never failing at any post of duty.

Candor compels the statement, he was not appre-

ciated by his Conference, nor was his worth even
known by the leaders in the Methodist Church. This
was clearly apparent the last years of his Conference
life. He would have made a fine presiding elder,
religious, efficient, thorough, evangelical, aggressive,
conservative. As good as was this man of God, he
would have been otherwise than human had he not
noticed in his own mind and keenly felt his non-
appreciation by his own Church in the character of
the appointments he received, but no one would have
discovered it by his utterances or by the manifestation of any ugly tempers.

While he was stationed at Sparta, the dancing
question was up, and much interest was felt in it.
This town, long under the direct influence of Bishop
Pierce, who lived nearby, was plain and simple in its ways, and had been entirely free from
this worldly evil. During Brother Dodge's pastorate, dancing had invaded the place, and had gotten
a foothold. Bishop Pierce scented evil afar off, and
sought an occasion to preach on the subject. It was
known what was coming; a large congregation was
present, and he did not spare this questionable worldly influence, but was very severe upon it. The
sermon, by the way, leaving out all local allusions,
has a place in a book of sermons of Southern Methodist preachers issued shortly thereafter by the Southern Methodist Publishing House. It created a stir
in the town, and if my recollection is not at fault, a
leading Methodist man, wealthy and influential in
the community, who had encouraged dancing in his

home, felt the rebuke very keenly, and withdrew from the church, joining another denomination. Brother Dodge took notes of that memorable sermon, and that year at White Oak Camp-meeting, gave the preachers in the tent a synopsis of it.

He was a fine general in a revival or holiness convention, such as was once held in Georgia. By common consent he was given the leadership, for he was a leader among leaders. He knew just what to do, and when to do it, when to close an altar service, as well as when to bring a meeting to a close. How he stands out in memory in those glorious by-gone meetings!

What an altar worker was he! No more efficient one could have been found. He hesitated not one moment to go to a penitent or a seeker after a clean heart when he presented himself at the altar. With his arms about him, he knew exactly what to say.

It will take the records of eternity to tell how many he helped in this way into the light of salvation. Peculiarly gifted in this respect, he used the gift for all it was worth, and God signally honored him. How his voice used to ring out as he would sing, "O mourner in Zion, how blessed art thou!" And that same voice now rings through the high arches of heaven in sweeter tones and in more triumphant strains. How he must revel in that world, forever saved, never more to go out again, with no one to oppose and none to try him!

Brother Dodge, though an intense believer in en-

5 d

tire sanctification, ever ready to advocate, explain and defend it, would never engage in controversy on the subject, nor deal in conversation merely to gratify curiosity.   Some good people might learn wisdom from his practice.   He was at White Oak Camp-meeting in 1879, and I also was present.   This Wesleyan doctrine was up, for he had preached upon it, and was known as a professor of this rich grace, for professors of, and believers in it at that time, were very rare. I ventured, in the preacher's tent, to ask him about it, not then knowing exactly what I wanted, nor clearly understanding myself.   He quietly told me if I was seeking truth, he would gladly talk with me, but not to gratify any curious questions or engage in a discussion over it.   Then we walked to the rear door, where he spoke of the subject in his own way.

In his later years, before his going away to heaven, I was about as close to him as most any other preacher.   I was on the inside while he was publishing the "Way of Life," that remarkable paper devoted exclusively to the doctrine of entire sanctification as taught by Wesley, and as enjoyed by Brother Dodge.   This periodical had a mission to fulfil, and right well did it fulfil that mission.   Few ever understood the labor, were aware of the great perplexity of mind, or even knew the fearful mental strain it cost to run it, for it was an individual concern, having no one back of it but Brother Dodge himself, with his limited resources.   He never made any money out of it, and had it not been for the fact that his wife and children did quite all the work, it would have been issued at a loss. In fact, it could not have been issued at all.

Sometimes I thought he was altogether too easy with delinquent subscribers, for be it known, hundreds of them never paid him a cent for the paper. Once I asked him to tell me candidly how many subscribers he had, and how much he realized in cash from his subscription-list. In round numbers he had at that time 6,000 subscribers, and did not receive more than $3,500, not quite fifty cents each, when the subscription price was $1.00 per year.

The financial strain he was often under was never known even by some of his best friends, growing out of this carelessness and injustice on the part of those who ought to have not only known better, but to have done better. And those unpaid subscriptions remain until this day. What will the judgment day have to do with them? Echo answers—what?

No one will ever know, besides his wife and his Lord, how much was upon him during those years. He was a busy pastor, an itinerant preacher, and that means much when time and strength are taken into account. He had the paper to look after—matter to get up, mailing to do, finances to arrange. Besides, his brethren, who did not know how to spare him, were constantly calling him to help in revival services, and he never knew how to refuse.

Often when at home working in the office of the paper, attending to correspondence, he would fall asleep at his desk, he was so completely exhausted. Sometimes I would presume to gently chide him, telling him he ought to hold up, go slow, and spare himself, lest he should break down. Even now, it is not altogether certain but that the labor, strain and overwork of those strenuous years tended to weaken his system and shorten his days.

While it was a positive loss to the cause of true holiness in Georgia, when he disposed of the "Way of Life," from which we have never recovered, yet it was somewhat of a relief to me when it was sold out, for our good brother was relieved of a burden altogether too heavy, which he had carried upon his head and heart for many years.

That paper, however, was dear to Brother Dodge's heart, and with it he did a work which was of untold benefit to the cause of holiness, as well as a great blessing to its subscribers. It did not live in vain, for upon its tombstone might well be written the inscription, "Blessed are the dead which die in the Lord, for their works do follow them." Well it is that there is an all-wise God, taking knowledge of His servants, who rewards men according to their works. Asbury Dodge's work on that little paper will not be overlooked in the final awards of the judgment day.

He was always careful of annoying any one, or of making unnecessary labor for others. The "Way of Life" was a movable publication. It went where its publisher went, and resided where he did. In 1885 he was sent to Gainesville. The paper went with him. On every publication day several large sacks of mail would go down to the Southern depot to be sent off. As a rule, it always struck the same train, with the same mailing force.

It is only fifty-three miles to Atlanta, and this large mail must be distributed while the train was between these two points. It got to be very burdensome to the railway mailing clerks, and not having the fear of God before their eyes, they would swear, and curse the paper and its publisher, publicly damning the "Way of Life" because of the increased burden put upon them. After awhile a brother who knew of this cursing, mentioned it to Brother Dodge.

Instead of declaring it was their duty to distribute whatever mail was put on the train, and they were paid for it, he quietly said he had never thought of the matter that way, that he would have the mail divided and sent to different trains, so as to make the burden easier on the hard-worked mail clerks, even though it might delay the paper a day. It was but the goodness of this man's heart breaking out into action.

A truer man never lived—true to his friends, true to his church, true to his convictions. We were together at a District Conference at McDonough in 1893, quartered at the same house, ate and slept together, and would walk to a near-by pond in which to bathe. What sweet converse we had together!

He was appointed to preach one day at 11 o'clock, by that other excellent man, now deceased, Rev. Thomas F. Pierce, then our Presiding Elder, a strong friend and admirer of Brother Dodge. What should he preach! Prayer and meditation settled his mind, and upon that subject so dear to his heart, sanctification, he spoke, and a strong sermon it was— clear, convincing, scriptural—from the text, Hebrews 13:12: "Wherefore, Jesus also, that he might sanctify the people with his own blood, suffered without the gate. Let us go forth, therefore, unto him without the camp, bearing his reproach."

Things said in that sermon remain with me till this day, especially his utterances about the reproach incident to the experience and profession of sanctification. In every age there was some point to which reproach attached. In Luther's day, it was justification by faith. In Wesley's time, it was the witness of the Spirit. Now it was sanctification. Few were the times the Lord was not consciously with Asbury Dodge when he preached, and this time he felt sensibly the Divine presence.

It was indeed a fortunate thing that men like A. J. Jarrell and W. A. Dodge were at the head of the Holiness movement in Georgia—fortunate for the Southern Methodist Church, when the fight was so intense upon this movement on the part of officials and individuals. The conditions were such at that time that a word from these two brethren would have carried hundreds of members into a separate organization. This was specially true of what is known as the Gainesville District, where at one time the fires of experimental godliness actually swept over this section of Georgia, during which some most remarkable things occurred.

A sanctified presiding elder was removed by the

appointing power, and another entirely out of sympathy with this doctrine took his place. A crisis was reached, and nothing but the loyalty of Dodge, Jarrell, and a few other leaders, held the people in the church. They never received any credit for it from the powers that be, but the Lord knows, and He will give credit where it is deserved.

He was one man who stood for years almost alone in the North Georgia Conference for the Wesleyan doctrine of entire sanctification, for he received it after earnest seeking, enjoyed it, lived it and professed it. Nobody who ever knew Asbury Dodge doubted he had what he claimed to possess. You might differ with him, you might not theoretically see it as he did, but you could not question the man's goodness and his devotion to God. Upon his conscience in a peculiar manner seemed to be laid the burden to confess definitely what the Lord had done for his soul in this second work of grace. Others might not have felt this as he did, but on all occasions when he told his experience, those who heard him were informed of the inward work done for him by the Sanctifying Spirit.

If I am not mistaken, he seemed to have once or twice lost this happy experience because he said he "failed to confess it." As he said, he had failed to take in the idea of the *"keeping power"* of this grace. At last he got hold of two passages which held him fast. First, with one foot, he stepped upon the promise, "Wherefore he is able to save unto the uttermost all that come unto God by him." Then placing the other foot of faith upon another, "Now unto him that is able to keep you from falling," he rested securely, and never afterward had occasion to doubt the grace received, or to mourn over its loss.

We were closely associated officially upon the Board of Church Extension, he being Treasurer, and I Secretary, and were thrown much together. It was at the Conference at Griffin, two months before he went to the good world. He was detained at home by the illness which afterward carried him away, and he was greatly needed in order to carry on our work. After some days' delay he put in his appearance, but no one will ever know what it cost him in strength and suffering to make the trip.

He sat at the table with me in the Conference-room enduring excruciating agony. At last he had to give up and return home. I was at the depot with him, and so intense was the pain he was suffering he had to get down on his knees while waiting for a delayed train. I helped him on board and put him in his seat, but immediately he had to again get on his knees on account of the agony he was enduring. I felt quite anxious about him making the trip home, for he had with him several thousand dollars of Church Extension money. But a merciful and protecting providence was over him, and he arrived at home safe, if not sound. No word of complaint ever escaped his lips, and beyond an occasional groan, no one would have suspected the suffering he was undergoing.

That was the last time I ever saw his glad face.

I shall see Asbury Dodge again, for I know where to find him. Farewell, thou friend of my life, till we greet each other on the other shore, where all are understood, and where a good God rewards his servants according to their works!

CLEMENT C. CARY,

North Georgia Conference.

Gainesville, Ga., June 28, 1906.

A NOTE FROM THE FIELD.

(Printed in Way of Life, March 15, 1893.)

Dr. F. E. Yoakum, Denver, Colorado, writes as follows: "I enclose you $2 to send the Way of Life to the following parties. The first named was converted in my office two weeks ago. He had brought his blind father-in-law to my office for consultation about his eyes. I asked the young man if he was a Christian. He replied, 'No, but I want to be.' 'How bad!' said I. 'Right bad,' he answered. 'Bad enough to get right down here in my office and ask God to give you a new heart?' 'Yes,' he replied. In less than two minutes he was converted and praising God. Praise the Lord!"

Note by Editor.—O for more M.D.'s after this sort!

A TRYING TIME TO OUR BROTHER.

One of the sorest trials which came into the life of our brother occurred in 1902, when he was at Second Church, Rome. In getting off the electric cars, his wife fell and broke her hip, from which she never entirely recovered, though she survives Brother Dodge. We will let her tell the story:

About our home, in Fourth Ward, Rome—it was one of the best and sweetest homes we ever had—the people all seemed to love us, and seemed as if they could never tire doing little kindnesses for us. We were both in perfect health all the year till October 10th.

On that day we went over into town to do some shopping, and while there Mr. Dodge heard that one of his stewards was sick, and we boarded the street-car to visit him. In some way, in getting off, I fell and broke my hip. It appeared as if the whole town knew it in quite a short while, and many came to see what they could do for us. The doctors, four in number, said it was a bad break, and that I would never walk again. I told Mr. Dodge to pray for me, for I knew the Lord would answer his prayer. I felt I would walk again. He prayed earnestly for God to lay his hand on the broken bone and heal it. In his prayer he said: "Lord, I know you can, and I believe you will." The Lord must have heard and answered him, for I never suffered but little with the break, and was not sick a minute during the seven weeks I was lying on my back in an iron frame. The eighth week Mr. Dodge moved me to Atlanta to my daughter's home, so my children could wait on me.

Christmas Day I walked with one crutch to the table to eat my dinner. So the Lord graciously heard my husband's prayers.

The Rome people could not have treated their own children better than they treated us.

A piece came out in the Rome paper after we left, bearing date of December 13, 1902, which is as follows:

"A TRIBUTE TO REV. W. A. DODGE.

"The Methodists of Rome are distressed at giving up Rev. and Mrs. W. A. Dodge, of the Second Methodist Church. As a mark of love for the pastor and his wife, a beautiful dinner was given on Thanksgiving Day in their honor by the Woman's Foreign Missionary Society of the Church."

A writer in one of the Rome papers pays this tribute to Mr. Dodge:

"The pure, simple gospel has been preached in all sincerity, tenderness and kindness every week. Hearts have been touched and lives quickened into activity which have hitherto been cold and dormant. Aside from this, bereaved hearts, over which the shadow of shadows has fallen, have been comforted by the message of the glorious resurrection from the lips of this consecrated man of God."

The only place Mr. Dodge ever spoke of wanting

to make a visit during his last illness, when he hoped
to get well, was to see friends in Rome. He told me
so at the Presbyterian Hospital where he was sick.
I said to him in reply that when we both got well we
would go to see our friends in that town. But God
ordered it otherwise. He went to see his friends
in heaven. God bless everybody in Rome.

    East Point, Ga.   Mrs. W. A. Dodge.

IN ROME, GEORGIA.

Rev. W. A. Dodge stayed only one year in Second Church, but that year counted for much to the
people there, for his influence abode long after he
left the charge. He had a very successful year, held,
I think, two meetings, kept in close touch with all
his members, and was greatly beloved. His influence
over a nephew of mine, was wonderful, and he was
most kind and helpful during much sickness in my
sister's family. This very naturally drew us all close
together, and shows what manner of man he was.

    I think his wife was one of the best women I ever
knew. When she was so severely injured by the
accident on the street-car, she bore her suffering
with great submission to the Divine will. As each
doctor came in that day, she asked immediately,
"Are you a Christian?" thus showing her interest in
things divine.

    I heard Brother Dodge say that one night on hear-
ing a noise in her room, he arose and went in, asking

her if she was suffering. She replied, "No, Mr. Dodge, I am praising God."

Rome, Ga. Mrs. H. D. Hill.

A LETTER FROM REV. W. A. DODGE.

Dear Clem: Conference comes on apace. Are you ready? Will you be ready? I would be glad if you would join me in prayer daily for our Conference, at its next session, and for our presiding Bishop. He will need Divine guidance, for he will not be able to get all the light he needs in the cabinet.

I do not know what will be done with poor Brother Blank. The odor of his case does not get any the less offensive. If his position could not hold him steady, I see nothing but shame and disgrace. There will possibly be those who will whitewash him if they can. I would rather be in heaven than in his place, by long odds.

That other once promising brother, ————, has settled his own case. He is here in the city. I see him occasionally. Poor fellow! I could weep over him. It is indeed sad. What a useful life his could be, and what evil his course will work with some people!

God bless you. Love to you both.

Yours in Jesus,

W. A. Dodge.

CONFERENCE MEMOIR.

The following memoir was prepared and read at the "Memorial Service," held at the North Georgia Annual Conference, at Marietta, Ga., in November, 1904:

William Asbury Dodge was born September 30. 1844, in Columbia County, Ga., near Harlem, and departed this life January 16, 1904, in East Point, Ga., after a lingering illness, in which he suffered intensely. He was soundly converted before he was fourteen years of age, was licensed to exhort on his sixteenth birthday and licensed to preach on his seventeenth birthday. He entered the Georgia Conference in 1862, was a chaplain in the Confederate Army, and spent more than forty years in the ministry.

In 1862 he was first married to Miss Henrietta Williams, of Oxford, Ga., who did not live very long thereafter. While he was on the Decatur Circuit, in 1867, she passed away. He was married the second time to Mrs. Mary Chandler, widow of Rev. W. B. Chandler, a local preacher, December 21, 1869, of DeKalb County, Ga. Four children were born unto them, three of whom survive.

As to what he was, let others who knew him speak:

The *Wesleyan Christian Advocate,* in noticing his death, said: "He was cheerful, active, robust, and from the date of entering the Conference, was effective and an efficient Methodist minister. He was a good preacher, scriptural, sensible, strong, and had rare gifts as a revivalist, and many souls through his ministry have been led to Christ and established in their religious lives."

Rev. George G. Smith says: "He ought to have been good. He had good parentage. His mother was a superior woman, of deep religious character. His father belonged to the sturdy New England stock, which gave the great philanthropist, Wm. E. Dodge, to the world. He lived up to his profession for thirty years, and never wavered in his adherence to his position, that there is a distinct second work of grace, called entire sanctification, to be reached now by faith instantaneously, and he became a leader in the movement which sought to further the work of holiness. Warm-hearted, benevolent, hospitable, upright, always ready for every good work, he had the full confidence of all who knew him. The godless recognized him as a good man who aimed all the time to lift up, and to comfort and direct in the right way. He was full of the Holy Spirit. It was his religion that made him good. He had learned much of the Divine Spirit, and of that gracious benediction called the 'fullness of God,' and religion to him was an abiding thing, and not something intermittent. The crowning fruit of the Spirit's indwelling is love, and his great heart overflowed with it. Toward his 'Holiness brethren' who were advocating and seeking to advance what he believed to be the highest truth, his heart went out in constant love, but toward all the Good Spirit made him affectionate, tolerant and kind. He was a true exemplar of the fruits of the Spirit, meek, patient, gentle, faithful. He always had a well spring of joy within. He was no time-server, no conformer with anybody, nor anything, in the matter of duty. He might have been mistaken as to what was right, but what he saw was true he was ready to die for. He fully believed the power of the gospel he preached. He was a great evangelist. He expected souls to be converted and Christians to be sanctified, and the fullness of his faith led him to dare great things and expect great things. He believed that God was willing to save sinners, and it was the most natural thing that they should be saved. Dear, warm-hearted Dodge! How sadly we will miss him!"

Brother Dodge thus speaks in some of his writings, of his religious experience after his conversion:

"In the fall of 1876, the second year of my pastorate at St. Paul's, Atlanta, my heart began to hunger for the blessing of entire sanctification. After earnest prayer for more than one hour, the Holy Spirit brought to my remembrance Hebrews 7:25: 'Wherefore He is able to save them to the uttermost that come unto God by Him, seeing He ever liveth to make intercession for them. I immediately said: 'Yes, there is a full salvation. I see it. He is my utmost Saviour and my Keeper, too,' and in a moment the storm was over, and the sweetest calm came into my soul. The work was done. I claimed the blessing and the keeping. On my way home, the Spirit said: 'Now will you tell it?' Satan said: 'What will your brethren say about it?' Then this passage came into my mind: John 5:44, 'How can ye believe which receive honor one of another, and seek not the honor that cometh from God only?' If they turn me out of the Church, I must and will confess what He hath done for my soul. This was April 15, 1876, at St. Paul's Church."

For twenty-eight years he enjoyed this rich religious experience, never doubting it for once, and humbly confessing it before men, and faithfully exemplified it to them.

Rev. W. H. Lloyd, formerly of the South Georgia Conference, has this to say:

"He was one of the purest, sweetest-spirited men that our Methodism has given to the world. He was truly a man who put his whole soul into his work. He was no self-seeker, nor was he ever triflingly employed. With all his earnest advocacy of entire sanctification, he never ignored nor abused the church, but on the contrary, co-operated in all her missionary, Church extension, and other benevolent enterprises to the fullest extent."

His brethren who labored with him in the Conference know this is true in every particular. At the time of his death he was the faithful and efficient Treasurer of the Board of Church Extension, and no man was truer to this interest of the Church, nor more faithful. His place was hard to fill.

6 d

With all his earnest advocacy of what he believed to be the Wesleyan view of holiness, he was tolerant of others, and no man can rise up and say he ever showed the slightest disloyalty to the Church of his choice, nor that he ever gave any encouragement whatever to division, schism, or "come-outism." He loved the Methodist Church, was true to his ordination vows, and gave the best part of his life to her ministry, ever going cheerfully without question where he was sent.

The life of this good man was far from being free from trials peculiar to the life of a Methodist itinerant. He was an excellent pastor, and sought to be true to the discipline of the Church. At one of his appointments, dancing had taken root among the membership, and Brother Dodge endeavored to administer judicious discipline at the time. As every preacher knows who has had to do this strange work, it is not pleasant, and he sought advice from Bishop Pierce, who wrote him a very tender and touching letter now preserved, in which this noble Bishop encouraged him in the course he was pursuing, and heartily endorsed him in seeking to rid the Church of dancing members.

The last hours of our departed and now glorified brother were full of thrilling interest. No terror of death was there. His death was one of the most triumphant, just such a death as we would have supposed Asbury Dodge to have died. On Thursday night before he left this world for the good world, he said to Rev. G. W. Matthews, one of his most intimate friends, as he went into the room to greet the dying man: "George, I am almost in heaven."

Calmly he viewed his approaching end, and said he believed God wanted him to go then—that he had prayed ever since God had given him children that he might live to see them grown and settled, and God had graciously granted his request, and he believed wanted him to go now. For four months preceding his departure for the skies, his prayer every day at family prayer was, "Lord, prepare us all for what Thou art preparing for us." His wife thought that prayer had particular reference to his next Conference appointment, but after Conference it was the same prayer. So when the last hour came, and his family had to give him up, then it was seen for what he had been so constantly praying, and that for which his Father had been preparing him.

When his ransomed spirit left the tenement of clay, for several minutes there was not a tear shed, for it seemed to those present that the very room was filled with the presence of angels.

Just before he breathed his last, his devoted and afflicted wife, holding him by the hand, asked him if he felt that the Lord Jesus was still with him. He bowed his head a moment, and promptly answered, "Yes, and He has been with me all the time." Showing deep interest in and concern for the wife of his bosom, he would forget himself, and when he would see a tear in her eye he would lift his hand and say, "Don't, don't."

His home life was indeed beautiful, and his devotion to the good woman who had so long stood by his side, the partner of his joys and sorrows, and the companion of his toils and travels, was indeed touching. Fourteen months before he died, his wife met with an accident in Rome, which made her an invalid for life, and she necessarily required much of his time and attention. No husband could have been more careful and attentive, and never for one moment did he ever grow weary in waiting upon and caring for her in her suffering and helplessness.

His wife bears testimony to this tender care and sincere devotion, for she says that during these long weary months he nursed her as if she were a baby. Once she said, "Mr. Dodge, don't you ever get tired?" and he quickly replied, "No, as long as you keep sweet, I never will grow tired waiting on you."

To her he would frequently repeat the precious promises of God's word, such as "My grace is sufficient for thee," "Cast thy burden upon the Lord and He will sustain thee," "I can do all things through Christ which strengtheneth me," while the last Scripture uttered by him, just before he went away to come back no more, was, "The blood of Jesus Christ, thy Son, cleanseth us from all sin."

He was fully aware his end was near, and acted as if he was just going away on a journey. About an hour before he died, he called his loved ones to him and bade them a final and affectionate farewell. He bade his loving and devoted wife good-bye, drew her down into his arms in an affectionate embrace, and then each one of his children, whom he embraced and bade farewell in turn, then the last, Wesley, the faithful colored man, who had been with the family for nearly twenty years, came for the final farewell, and he. too, was clasped by the dying, triumphant man of God, to whom death had no sting and grave no victory. And thus he left them to meet them again in heaven, whither he has gone. With his benediction falling upon those about his dying couch, he gathered up his feet, and quietly fell asleep in Jesus, just outside the gates of the celestial city, to awake the next moment in the home of the good.

CLEMENT C. CARY.

The Conference history of Rev. W. A. Dodge is as follows:

1862, November, admitted on trial.

1863, Watkinsville Circuit, Junior preacher.

1864-1865, Chaplain in Confederate Army.

1865, January, ordained Deacon by Bishop Pierce.

1866, December, ordained Elder by Bishop McTyeire.

1867, 1868 and 1869, Decatur Circuit.

1869, Atlanta City Mission.

1870, Evans' Chapel and Mission, Atlanta.

1871, Dahlonega Circuit.

1872 and 1873, Presiding Elder Dahlonega District.

1874, Presiding Elder, Gainesville District.

1875 and 1876, St. Paul's, Atlanta.

1877 and 1878, Sparta.

1879, 1880, 1881, 1882, Eatonton.

1883, Atlanta City Mission.

1884, Boulevard and Exposition Mills Mission, Atlanta.

1885, Gainesville.

1886, Cartersville.

1887, Fulton Circuit.

1888, Supernumerary.

1889, Junior preacher, Walker Street, Atlanta.

1890, Forsyth Circuit.

1891, Bolton Circuit.

1892, Conference Colporteur.

1893, Walker Street, Atlanta.

1894, South Atlanta Mission.

1895, 1896, 1897, Supernumerary.

1898, 1899, 1900, 1901, East Point.

1902, Second Church, Rome.

1903, St. James,' Atlanta.

1904, Fairburn.

Just in proportion as we die to this world do we live in His resurrected life. "He that will lose his life for my sake shall find it." We never have complete victory until we forsake all for Him. Luke 13:14. Let us separate ourselves from sin and die with Him to the spirit of the world, and through Him rise in newness of life to victory over the world, the flesh and the devil.

MY IMPRESSIONS OF REV. W. A. DODGE.

I first met Rev. W. A. Dodge in Atlanta at Rev. A. G. Haygood's, I think it was in the fall of 1866. If memory serves me correctly, he was then on the Stone Mountain circuit. He seemed so cheerful, glad and happy in his work, that I almost envied him. We were near the same age, perhaps he was two years my senior. I think with us both, it was love at first sight, for we ever afterwards loved one another, and sometimes when he met me he would shout, and my heart would leap for joy at the very grasp of his hand.

In the year 1871 we were on adjoining circuits in the mountains of North Georgia. We worked together that year, especially in our camp-meetings. At the great Lumpkin camp-meeting he was beset by an almost unconquerable temptation, but he obtained the victory like a man of God. I saw him just about the time the victory came. Oh, what gladness and rejoicing filled his heart, and how, with his tongue, he gave glory to God!

The years rolled on, and "The Holiness Movement," as it was called, reached out over the North Georgia Conference. I do not know the circumstances under which he claimed the blessing of full salvation, I only know that he was one of the first men who deeply impressed me, in the midst of the great revival. As preacher, pastor, evangelist and editor of "The Way of Life," he threw himself into

the work with a zeal that was absolutely quenchless.
I always enjoyed his preaching. It was to me scriptural, clear, and powerful. He preached almost from
sea to sea, and everywhere he went his name became as a household word, and now that he has gone
his memory is like precious ointment, poured forth.

At the holiness convention held in Griffin, Ga., in
the Methodist church, in the spring of 1882, the next
morning, after the opening of the meeting in the
afternoon, I went early to the church, and met a con-
siderable number of the brethren, who came before
the services to pray and praise. I was standing at
the organ, helping to sing, when Brother Dodge entered the door, and walked swiftly down the aisle,
with his usual elastic step. Without saying "good-
morning," or giving any usual greeting, he threw
his arms around me and began to shout. How long
he rested his head on my shoulder and praised God, I
do not now recall. I only remember that the Pente-
cost of the day began to fall on us, and it was almost like "fire and the sound of a rushing mighty
wind."

I followed him in his pastorate at Cartersville,
and with the truly devoted and spiritual membership
of the church and town, I never served a people who
had been better trained in the doctrines of Methodism and of the Bible, and who received more gladly
the word of God.

The last time I saw Brother Dodge was in the
Presbyterian Hospital, in Atlanta. The end was
not far off, but he was lying there with his daugh-

ters each holding his hands, and he was talking of salvation, Jesus and heaven, and was thanking God for his Christian daughters.

I would have been among the mourners at his funeral, but I was in the midst of one of the greatest meetings of my life, and the news of his death came a day too late.

We shall rarely, if ever, see his like again. We loved like David and Jonathan. Some sweet day we shall walk together with Jesus, in white, with the blood-washed on the other shore.

B. E. L. TIMMONS,
North Georgia Conference.

Atlanta, Ga., May 25, 1906.

LIFE OF MILLER WILLIS.

(An advertisement from Way of Life, March 8, 1893.)

The Life of this Holy Ghost, fire-baptized Layman can be had for only ONE DOLLAR.

It is a benediction to read it. He was a living illustration of the power and blessedness of "Full Salvation."

Address with the cash,

REV. W. A. DODGE,
48 Stonewall St., Atlanta, Ga.

SOME INTERESTING INCIDENTS.

My first knowledge of Rev. W. A. Dodge was when he was sent to Sparta, Ga., in 1879. A meeting was going on at Culverton, five miles distant, and he came out to help. He did not preach the day I was there, but was called on to pray. I was very much impressed with the prayer. He seemed to be so full of the Spirit that not only myself, but all present, felt that a man very near to God was in our midst. Mr. Waller, of the Methodist church, a man of ripe religious experience, said he did not know when he had been so stirred in his soul as during that prayer.

I was sent to the Dawsonville circuit, for my first appointment. I had him to come to Lumpkin Camp-meeting that year. I sent my horse and buggy to Gainesville for him. The road was hilly, had several creeks and two rivers to cross—no bridges then. The horse brought him and his baggage through safely. When he got to the campground he said: "Your horse must be a consecrated animal—he was faithful on all parts of the road." I told him he was "on the altar to haul preachers to meetings."

The people, by hundreds, came to hear him. His preaching, praying, singing, and personal work, were signally owned of God. It was a marvelous meeting. Nearly every tent became an altar where souls were saved. Many entered the experience of perfect love, and to this day they talk of that revival. I received about fifty into the church at Lumpkin, and the fire started there and swept all over the mountain country. Brother Dodge could be heard at midnight praying for some one seeking pardon or purity.

He was the instrument of leading many preachers into the experience of "perfect love." Many would attend the Holiness Conventions, and would be impressed with his fervent spirit, joyful experience, and untiring zeal, and be led to seek for perfect love. How he rejoiced to welcome a colaborer into the experience of a triumph over all sin!

He was a power at all the meetings; his theme was the promoting of holiness. He wanted a work of grace that would take out the last remains of sin.

I have seen him crawling on his knees from one to another in the slums of Atlanta, praying that God would give the poor sinners clean hearts, that they might be able to resist the temptations peculiar to their class. I believe that Peters street, Atlanta, felt his power as it did no other preacher, and his Mission there did more to purify the moral atmosphere than anything that had been done. The police force of the city have some idea what he did to make their work lighter in the slum district.

I was with him during his revival at Eatonton. It was a great meeting. The town was stirred from side to side. To show what a heart of love and sympathy he had for the sinner—a young lady came into the sitting-room at the parsonage one morning, all broken down under conviction. She threw herself on her knees, and asked him to pray for her. I never heard such pleading for a sinner. He reached the ear of God, and she arose with her face radiant with the glow of God's love. I believe he took more pleasure in leading a soul to God than any man I ever saw.

Rev. W. A. Dodge and Rev. George H. Patillo, deceased, were close friends in the ministry. Brother Pattillo began his meeting at Smyrna, of the Culverton circuit, and had Brother Dodge to assist him. His preaching moved the people as no other up to that time, as far as my knowledge goes. Numbers were converted and the church, which was supposed to be dead, took on new life, and the effects lingered for years. As one of the results, two preachers are itinerants in the North Georgia Conference.

I soon saw that he was a God-appointed evangelist. His preaching, exhortations and altar work were marvelous in power and production.

JOHN H. LITTLE,
North Georgia Conference.

Atlanta, Ga.

THE HARDEST FIELD AND THE GREAT-
EST VICTORY.

Yes, dear Brother Dodge was in Eatonton several
years—four, I think—and, as I see it, after an in-
terval of over twenty years, he did a greater work in
this town than any other pastor since the civil war.

The parsonage in which I now live was built by
him, and when I first came, and made some criticism
of some parts of the house, a good woman replied:
"It was built by dear Brother Dodge, one of the
best men who ever lived, who is in heaven now, we
all hope and believe." I said very little more about
the house, for my mind and heart were turned toward the memory and the present abode of this man
I loved so dearly.

His picture hangs in a frame on the wall of the
parsonage, with those of former pastors at Eatonton. It is in my study, the same room he used for
his study, and I often refer to it and to him in my
preaching.

One of the brethren told me last year that at first
Brother Dodge could not have a meeting here till
he turned out of the church some of the members
who were not living right. Then the Lord graciously gave him a revival, and, from what I learn,
nearly all who had been expelled came back, while
numbers of sinners were converted and joined the
church. All of which proved that the judicious ad-

ministration of discipline did not hurt the church, but helped it.

Sister Dodge once told me, when they first came to Eatonton, they had a hard time. Many men antagonized Brother Dodge because he opposed sin. But he began a meeting, was greatly burdened, and got the promise of Rev. Sam Jones to help him. Brother Jones came, and the power of God rested upon the services. It was not long till men who had been hating Brother Dodge came, with weeping eyes and broken hearts, and threw their arms around his neck and asked his pardon for having wronged him, and begged for his prayers. "When a man's ways please the Lord, He maketh even his enemies to be at peace with him." The meeting was a great one, and moved and swept the town.

Since I have been here, men of fine sense and good judgment have told me that Brother Dodge was the cause largely of prohibition winning in Putnam county. He championed this just cause with such invincible determination that it is generally conceded he was the main agent in the success of the contest. So it appears to me at this day that prohibition here is a standing monument to the faith and prayers, the push and power of W. A. Dodge.

The Chairman of my Board of Stewards has a son, about twenty years of age, named for Brother Dodge. He graduated in dentistry a few days ago in Atlanta, and doubtless will settle here, to follow his profession. Brother Dodge is also living in many other families in Eatonton, in name, in love and in character.

One of my best men, J. C. Reid, a steward, and for several years Sunday-school superintendent, was converted during the pastorate of Brother Dodge. He once dissipated much, and was a leading sinner in the town, who tried in every way to shun the preacher as much as possible. One day in passing the parsonage, Brother Dodge came out and meeting him cordially, began to talk to him about his soul, and got him to promise to "come out to meeting." He came, and, like Saul of Tarsus, the Lord met him there, convicted him pungently, and he was gloriously converted. Brother Reid is a good man, and is another monument to the work of W. A. Dodge.

A man living out in the country, in talking to me last year about one of the Methodist churches in the county, said that the best meeting ever held in that church in a long time was conducted there by J. C. Reid when Rev. T. A. Seals was on the circuit.

This gives but a very meager idea of the work and the influence of Rev. W. A. Dodge during the years Providence put him in Eatonton.

FRANK S. HUDSON,
Pastor Eatonton Methodist Church.

Eatonton, Ga., June 2, 1906.

A VOICE FROM THE PAST.

Here is a voice long silent in death, of one who was loved and esteemed by the entire church, which bears testimony to the fidelity of Rev. W. A. Dodge, and shows conclusively that our much loved departed Bishop, George F. Pierce, was in perfect accord with all disciplinary efforts to rid the church of dancing.

Brother Dodge was stationed in Eatonton at the time, and was having trouble with wordly-minded, dance-loving church members. He was seeking to enforce discipline against them, a lost art in the present day Methodist church, and had requested Bishop Pierce to come and preach for him. The following letter is in answer to that request, and shows the heart of that great man of God. After so many years it affords fine reading:

"Sparta, Ga., February 8, 1881.

"My Dear Brother: Oh! that I could be with you next Sunday! But my throat will not bear preaching just now. I have been vocally out of fix all this bad weather.

"I hope you will stand firmly by the Discipline in dealing with your disorderly members. The Church must stop this trifling with her rules. I am more than ever convinced that dancing professors know nothing even of the first principles of Christ's religion. No one in the enjoyment of religion ever danced since the world was made. No loving, self-denying, obedient Christian ever will. The whole thing as now carried on is of the earth earthly, sensual and devilish. The Church can not allow it. Those who will not give up this and kindred sins must go out by withdrawal or expulsion. The Church of God can not be a saloon for the children of the devil. They must go where they belong.

"I can not find the Journals you ask for. But the General Conference did interpret the General Rule to forbid all dancing—round and square, private and public. The Bishops were directed to say so in the pastoral address. The testimony of the Church against dancing has been uniform and steady and unequivocal all along. All the churches have denounced it as sinful and corrupting.

"All the people in the Church who indulge in this ungodly pastime violate their baptismal vows, ignore Church authority, grieve their pastors, sin against God, and disgrace their Christian profession. Oh! Shame—shame—shame!

"I thank God for His grace to you. I like the way you talk. God fill us always with all spiritual benediction and grace. My heart swells in sympathy with you. I love God and the Church, I hope, with a pure heart fervently. I pant for all the fullness of God. I never profess great things, but I am ready to confess Jesus in His life and death, and power to save. May He save us unto the uttermost.

"Ann joins me in love to you and Sister Dodge and the children. God bless you all evermore.

"Affectionately,

"G. F. PIERCE."

7 d

FROM A DISTANCE.

In the summer of 1885, August, I think, I attended a camp-meeting at Murdock, Ill. Holiness was the theme of the many evangelists and workers from many States. Many scenes of interest were witnessed, and the Holy Ghost was present in mighty power. One scene never forgotten by the writer occurred here, such as I have never seen repeated through years of service in revival and camp-meetings, which I will give.

Brother Dodge, whose face was beaming with holy love and light, plead that the Spirit's voice might not be quenched, and that those who heard Him calling for service, might right then, resist no longer, but say "yes" to God. Instantly a young married woman, the wife of a Quaker minister, sprang to her feet and began telling how she had resisted the call of the Spirit to preach the gospel, because it was not popular for women to preach, although her church licensed and believed in women prophesying. Just as she said, "I resist no longer, I will obey the call," the fire of the Holy Ghost apparently fell on the whole audience. Instantly some were shouting, others fell where they were praying, and holy pandemonium reigned. Immediately another call was made, and such a turning to the Lord I have never seen repeated.

The writer had heard the call for years, and up to that time was walking in all the light she had.

During the same meeting, before this incident occurred, while Brother Dodge was pleading for us to "say yes to God," he paused and said: "If God should call any of you to work in the South, would you be willing to go?" Then we went to prayer and were earnestly urged by Brother Dodge to examine our hearts and walk in the light of the Spirit's illumination.

I shall never forget that moment; conscious of being wholly surrendered to God and filled with His Spirit, my life, filled as it was with active service for church and home, seemed to pass before me like a panoramic scene. I loved my church work so much it seemed for an instant impossible that God would want me to give it up. But the still, small voice urged, "Will you go to the Southland?" I said, "Yes, Lord, anywhere Thou leadest." I was conscious of this step being an unusual one for me, but knew it was the voice of the Spirit. A quietness and an assurance of being in complete abandonment to His will then came, which was wonderful. A few months later a door opened for my going South, and I was not disobedient to this call, but with careful steps and Divine testings I obeyed. After all these years, during which I have spent a number in the Southern field, I can say it was a Divine call, attended by my Saviour's approbation.

Mrs. Amy Cooper had been taking Brother Dodge's paper, "The Way of Life." I subscribed for it, and continued taking it until it was merged into "The Methodist," then the "Pentecostal Herald," not missing a single year.

Several years afterward I received a letter from Mrs. Cooper, stating that she and her husband studied and preached together, and at that time she was at a fashionable watering place in California, and, by request of the people, filled her husband's pulpit, he having died a few months before.

I have not heard from her since, but expect to meet up there, bringing sheaves for Him whom we serve.

MRS. R. E. DIMMITT,

Evangelist of Illinois Holiness Association, Springfield, Ill.

Griggsville, Ill.

Ten things necessary in a pure life:

Live a pure life.

Hearing before judging.

Thinking before speaking.

Harboring clean thoughts.

Standing by your principles.

Being generous to an enemy.

Stopping your ears to gossip.

Bridling a slanderous tongue.

Being square in business dealings.

Putting the best construction on the acts of others.

SEVERAL THINGS OF INTEREST.

Rev. William Asbury Dodge was one of the purest men I ever knew. Sincerity was a prominent trait in his character. No one ever suspected him of self-seeking, or place-hunting, in his appointments in the Conference. He was fully given to the Lord in every phase of his work.

As Presiding Elder and pastor, he and I were in close relationship. He never intimated to me anything of his preference as to appointments. He was stationed in Gainesville in 1885, and it was the desire of the people that he should succeed me on the Gainesville district, and I urged his appointment to the district, that he might continue the revival work then in progress throughout the district. However, Bishop Wilson did not agree with me, and appointed Rev. A. G. Worley.

It was known to all that Brother Dodge professed entire sanctification, according to the Wesleyan and Bible doctrine. He lived up to what he professed, and preached up to what he lived. He was a large factor in what was called the "Holiness Movement" in the Gainesville district and other parts of Georgia. He seemed to have settled it that his lot was with the holiness movement, and, like Moses, was willing to suffer for his choice.

He and Revs. A. J. Jarrell and W. C. Dunlap were a trio in the evangelistic work of "spreading Scriptural holiness over these lands." Some of the

Bishops and most of the prominent men of the North
Georgia Conference were opposed to this doctrine,
and consequently opposed to those who were behind
the movement. This opposition was demonstrated
in the character of many appointments made.
Whether Brother Dodge's appointments were up to
his ability or not, he always went uncomplainingly
to his work, and did all he could to bring the people
up to a higher plane of Christian living.

Whatever extremes there may have been in the
preaching and methods of Brother Dodge and others
on what was called the "holiness line" (and there
was far less than was charged), there was certainly,
and beyond all doubt, the power of God in the movement.

In the year 1885, when Brother Dodge was stationed in Gainesville, and he, Bros. Jarrell, Dunlap,
Miller Willis, and others, were preaching holiness
over Northeast Georgia, and great spiritual power
was in the churches, there were added to the Gainesville District that year, on profession of faith, thirteen hundred and sixty-five souls; while six hundred
and fifty additions was the next highest in districts
nearly twice as large in membership. "By their fruits
ye shall know them."

If the dignitaries of the church had joined in the
movement, and had had the same baptism of power
these men had, and, if necessary, had eliminated
what was thought to be extreme in the movement,
there would have been, I verily believe, a different
state of things in the church at this day.

Ever since the decline of that movement the church papers, and many of the pastors, have been lamenting the want of power and success that attended the ministry of Brother Dodge and others wherever they preached.

Whether at the Scottsville Camp-meeting in Texas or the Indian Springs Camp-meeting in Georgia, or in his regular pastoral work, Brother Dodge had a great zeal for souls. In editing "The Way of Life," and in his consistent Christian life, and his zealous evangelistic work of so many years, doubtless few, if any, ever led more people to Christ and encouraged so many in the Christian life.

Brother Dodge was not only a successful soul-winner, but he was one of the most lovable of men. His brethren of the Conference, as well as all who knew him, loved him.

He, Bros. Jarrell, Dunlap, Miller Willis, and many others, with whom the writer stood shoulder to shoulder for many years, have passed over to their reward, and he to the margin is come, "willing to stay—ready to go."

W. A. PARKS,

North Georgia Conference.

Whitesburg, Ga., June 2, 1906.

PLEASING RECOLLECTIONS.

W. A. Dodge! Did I know him? Can I speak a word concerning him?

That beautiful passage from the Pacific Ocean to the magnificent bay on which lovely San Francisco was built is called the "Golden Gate." Sheened by the morning and evening sun, this passage ripples into golden laughter. It is *golden,* in that it is the passage to safety to every storm-pursued craft; it is *golden,* in that it brings daily a wealth of business prosperity to the lap of this queen of the West; it is *golden,* in that it admits to our hospitable shores all the world, who seek bread or who look for the Christ; and is *golden,* in that it passports to "all the world" every man and woman to whom God has given a charge, to the "regions beyond." Such, to my mind, was Brother Dodge to the "Holiness Movement," in the South in general, and Georgia in particular.

My attention was first called to him when he was a pastor in Eatonton, Georgia. I heard of how he laid siege to that little town; of how he would fast and pray; crying to God all night. Of how days in advance of victory he got the assurance, and would come in and say, "O wife, God has given us the city, God has given us the city." He had, too, for that was Eatonton's great revival.

Who that ever looked into his face doubted its transformed character. The serenity of faith, the

joy of faith, the innocence of faith, the friendship
of faith, the victory of faith, played over his great,
honest face like the kaleidoscopic tides of the Golden
Gate, breaking in innocent consciousness against the
water-guards of some great ocean palace in the setting sun of a crimson November.

I often met Brother Dodge, in counsel and in a
number of campaigns, often preaching side by side
with him. Candor compels me to say he was closer
to me than I was to him. There was reason for this.
He was so transparent that you knew him and trusted
him at once. The dangers which I scented, and often
spoke of in those days, were not seen, suspected or
feared by him. It was all bright to his bright faith
and glowing experience. I have heard him expound
the Word until I said, "I see Jesus in those doctrines."
I have heard him sing "Is not this the Land of Beu-
lah?" until the lilies of the land intoxicated me; the
grapes of Eschol fell in showers from the branches
above, and the pomegranates rolled in profusion,
while the dews of Hermon cooled me, and I said
Christ is singing in my very soul. I have heard him
tell his experience until I felt like saying I was mistaken. Christ is not so much in those great doctrines, nor in that heaven-born, heaven-sung song,
but the great Christ, the all-Christ, lies in a deep
experience. Then I have turned and looked on him.
Centripetal and centrifugal fires surged through my
soul, while I exclaimed, "O, I was mistaken, for there
is the Lord of my life, the Christ of my own cruci-
fixion, the Saviour of my own soul, sitting in holy

transfiguration on the face of Asbury Dodge!"
Hanging my head in confusion I have sobbed out,
"O, my Lord, to shine like that, even in glory, would
be much!"

I have not known much of him for the last twelve
years of his life, but am not concerned, for the dia-
mond returns not to charcoal.

J. B. CULPEPPER,

Evangelist.

June 25, 1906.

TENDER MEMORIES.

As memory unrolls the scroll of the past, some faces and figures, some times and places, stand out upon the canvas thereof as do pictures upon the walls of our homes. How strange, and yet how true it is, that one will thus have one person indelibly stamped, and another will have another!

Just so, dear reader, it was that Rev. W. A. Dodge impressed this humble handmaiden of the Lord from the first Sunday that she ever spent on Indian Springs Holiness Camp-ground, some years since. In company with dear Aunt Hodges, of blessed memory, I was passing a small canvas tent, when awful groans were heard. My companion remarked, "Brother Dodge is sick there," and stopped to inquire after the sufferer. Involuntarily I raised my eyes for a moment, and beyond the forms of those speaking together in the tent door I caught a glimpse of two muscular arms grasping a small oak around which the tent was built, to which he was clinging, so excruciating were his sufferings.

Brother J. B. Culpepper led the night service, and the meeting preceding it was led by dear Dr. Godbey, of Kentucky. At the conclusion Brother Culpepper called for any physician in the audience to meet him just outside the Tabernacle, and I felt sure that it was for Brother Dodge. How my heart went down before God for the sufferer, for many had spoken to me of his pure and useful life!

A year later I met him under that same Tabernacle pouring out his heart for the Church—the Church, not the world—his arms extended, as in agony he pleaded. Immediately there came into my mind the Saviour's words, "O Jerusalem, Jerusalem, how oft would I have gathered thee as a hen doth gather her brood under her wings, and ye would not," and there was in them a far deeper meaning than ever before, for if a man could feel for the Church what this man evidently felt, no wonder that the Saviour of the world, "being in an agony, prayed the more earnestly."

Each succeeding year found us both, and, for the most part, our families, at the dear camp-ground. How joyously each family hailed the coming of the other!

He seldom (many felt too seldom) preached at Indian Springs Camp-meeting; for he was busy always with its many interests, to which he ever gave close and constant attention.

Well do I remember one year especially, when it seemed that all the powers of darkness were in full battle array against God and all that the camp-ground stood for! Loving, yet firm, brave, true and strong, Brother Dodge was here, yonder, every-where when most needed. Always the same sancti-fied personality, whether preaching, praying, exhort-ing sinners to give their hearts to God, or witnessing in a court of justice against those same sinners, it was impossible to forget Brother Dodge.

In the spring of 1897 or 1898 he and Brother G.

W. Mathews held a joint session of the North and South Georgia Holiness Associations in Lovett, Ga., at that time a small whiskey-soaked town (what it is now, God knoweth), in Laurens county, Ga. How those sinners had sneered, boasted and criticised the idea of such a meeting in their town! But God came with the preachers, and to all eternity many will rejoice that God sent such power into their midst, as is referred to in Acts 1:8: "But ye shall receive power after that the Holy Ghost is come upon you."

Lovett being near our town of Garbutt, our people attended the services at night almost en masse.

Saturday night, in the quietude of my own home, God called on me to perform one of the most difficult tasks for Him I had ever yet done, to wit, to talk the next night to a negro District Conference on "Personal Piety and Power." This was just a short time after the Palmetto tragedy.

I shall never forget Brother Dodge's words of cheer and encouragement: "Yes, do it by all means, Sister Garbutt, for the only way to grow in grace steadily is to enter every door of opportunity that the Lord opens for you." I followed his advice then, and have followed it ever since, with victory in my soul as a result.

The working man's attire, with carpenter's tools in hand, seemed just as fitting as broadcloth and a pulpit for this man of God.

The last Indian Springs Camp-meeting which he attended he came to our cottage, and, asking for every member of the family, wanted to know if any of us objected to his building his cottage next door to ours. My first thought was, "As if we could object to living next door to the angels!"

Elsewhere in these papers will be found the personal, written consecration of himself and his all to God.

Mrs. Callahan (Annie Pierce) his baby, then unborn, says she has always considered herself a part of that consecration.

Sister Dodge tells of it this way: They were boarding with an elegant Presbyterian lady, who seemed always to regard Brother Dodge as a paragon of goodness. Of the day of which he writes, she says: "He was in the Church study, and did not come home to dinner. I sent Attie and the nurse for him. Attie came back, saying, 'Mamma, I can't make papa hear me. He is walking the floor, singing and crying. He won't hear me.'

"I said to the lady, 'He is so anxious about the Church he is almost crazy.' She said, 'Don't say anything to him, Mary, he is so good he wants everybody else to be good.' I knew it was himself he was anxious about, but was ashamed to tell her, for I, too, thought him as good as he could be, but soon saw the mistake, as he was so much better afterward. We had company that day, and I being proud of my good-looking husband, wanted them to see him, as my pride was wounded. In about two weeks I sought, and he helped me to find, the same blessing. Then what power, joy and love attended us everywhere!"

I only pause to say I wish each reader of these pages could have been at the Indian Springs Holiness camp-ground last year, the day his dear ones took possession of the lovely little cottage next door to mine, where loving hands had already spread the noonday meal, sent in from the various tents, as a small token of love to the "Mother of our camp-ground," their children and grandchildren.

God help you and me, dear reader, to seek the truth, walk in the light, and die in the faith, as did W. A. Dodge.

Mrs. S. S. Garbutt.

Wright, Ga., June 23, 1906.

THREE SOULS TOUCHED BY THIS MAN OF GOD.

Some twenty years ago, or less, among the hills of North Georgia there dwelt a youth. He was in no special sense a paragon of goodness, of badness, or indifference, so far as spiritual things go.

He sometimes attended church, usually on "big meeting" occasions, quarterly conferences, and perhaps the neighborhood "singings," taught usually by a master of the character note system, who generally made up his class to take in two Sundays. What a happy week for young folks! Lots of rides, many walks, much "sweethearting," and plenty of merry chatter among young and old, as they gathered in the morning at the designated school-house or church; or at "recess" went to the nearby well for nature's own remedy for many ills, the cool, limpid water; or in season cut the lovely luscious watermelon, brought in plenty from their homes.

In those days folks, especially the young, were more willing to go long distances to gatherings than at the present day, nor were they quite so fastidious as to the mode of travel. Carriages, buggies, wagons, ox-carts, with a good sprinkling of youngsters who rode horseback or came on foot, made up, as a rule, "the big meeting" or "all day singing" congregation.

Well, a youth who had scarcely attained as yet

his majority, attended a revival, was deeply convicted and gloriously converted.

Soon after this he heard that Rev. W. A. Dodge,
a sanctified itinerant minister, would preach at a
certain place on a certain day. Wondering what
manner of man this was, he determined that the
plow should stand still in the field and the horse remain in the stall, while he walked the intervening
space of some miles to find him out.

It so chanced that the young man got there first,
and at last among the arrivals he saw a lone man
drive up, get out of the buggy, and as he tied his
horse this youth was mightily convinced, before the
preacher had spoken a word, that this man had
something in his soul which he himself did not have,
but greatly needed.

It seems almost useless to add that just a little
preaching, just a little teaching, just a little explain-
ing of the way, and that young man's hungry soul
was filled with the Holy Ghost and with power and
he went away on fire for God and has all these years
been mightily used of Him, having wisdom such as
no earthly seminary can impart, and knowledge not
born of this world. East or west, 'tis just the same
—a mighty lifting up of Christ in heart and life and
pulpit, and, as is promised, a wondrous drawing to
Him.

While in Americus recently I learned how our
dear Vashti Blasingame Home and School idea of
management was born in the heart of a dear little
woman who sat under the Tabernacle at Indian

8 d

Springs Camp-ground one stormy Sunday evening and heard Brother Dodge preach. As he expounded the word, and the elements warred without, the Spirit warred within her soul. Finally she made the consecration, and got that blessed experience:

"There's a deep settled peace in my soul,
Tho' the billows of sin near me roll,
He abides, Christ abides."

And she assured me that from that day there had been unbroken peace and constant abiding.

Nor can I forget the day or cease to give God the glory for the fact my own little daughter came into the same experience during one of the few sermons he preached there. She possibly met him on the "golden shore," having preceded him home some time.

MRS. S. S. GARBUTT.

Wright, Ga.

HIS EXPERIENCE AS RECORDED BY HIMSELF.

I have taken this method to keep in remembrance important items of my Christian experience. I have often felt that I needed a deeper work of grace in my heart.

I have twice sought "perfect love," and twice I lost it. Once, and the first time, in 1870, in the latter part of September, I walked moment by moment in the light of God's favor, until about the middle of the month of April, 1871, when I lost it. I continued thus until about the middle of May, 1873, when I sought more deeply the work in my own heart, making a complete consecration verbally to God, and again I was made happy in love.

I continued thus until the month of August, 1874, and this time I felt that God, for sin, not overt and damning, but sin nevertheless, again withdrew from me the light of His countenance, and I continued in this state for twelve hours, when again I felt that all was peace, and continued so for about a month. But I fell to doubting at the remembrance of my sin, and again the light went out, and in this state I remained until April, 1875.

At the Conference in the winter of 1874 I was taken off the Gainesville District and put in charge of St. Paul's station in the city of Atlanta. I passed the first of this year with no very bright manifestation of God's presence and love in my heart. Often cast down, and preaching without any distinct sense of Divine presence.

On the first Sunday night in the month of April I began a protracted service in the church. It continued for more than a week without any visible manifestation of God's presence. My own heart was cold. The church was like a floating Greenland iceberg, and sinners as hard as adamant.

I began to turn my eyes within, and under the light of God's Spirit I felt that I needed to be washed—my own self, for there was much of the carnal mind remaining. So on the 8th of this month I sat down and did what I never did before, namely, to make a written deed of myself to God, with all I had. This is about the sum it—(for after signing it I sealed it up, and desire that it remain sealed until after I am dead)—that I consecrate myself to God, mind, soul and body, time, influence, wife and two children, Wesley Atticus and May Belle, books, clothes, property, all—yes, all that I have on the earth now, or ever will have.

This is about the sum of it. After writing it out, I got down on my knees and prayed God in mercy, for Jesus' sake, to have respect unto my poor offering, for I felt that it was so poor that nothing but mercy could move Him to accept it, and on my knees, in His presence, I signed it, put it in an envelope and sealed it up. I looked every minute for God to come and accept the offering, and, blessed be His name, He did not keep me long in waiting.

On Friday, April 9th, the day following, in the

study of the church, about half-past twelve o'clock, I felt that God sent His fire and consumed the offering. I felt that He went through me and cleansed my poor soul from all sin, and oh! what views I had of Jesus, such as I never had before.

I went to the congregation with new light and addressed them, and God began to approve by convicting the church, and others began to seek, and still the work went on.

But my own experience is that now, moment by moment, I look up to Jesus to cleanse me and keep me clean. I am sometimes overwhelmed with the glory of His presence. At other times I am filled with such heavenly tranquility, and now my constant prayer is, "Jesus keep me," and Jesus does, for His is the power to do it.

On Sunday, the 18th, I sounded the alarm to Zion that "without holiness no man shall see the Lord," and God came in mighty power upon us, and His people sought and found. It will soon be three weeks, and God is still moving on the church.

April 24th. Yesterday was a day of no powerful display of Divine presence, but I feel that God is doing for me now what the cold winter does for the forest timber after months of growth—"hardening."

I feel that I am being established in the way of Christianity as never before.

April 27th. Saturday last was a day long to be remembered. The four o'clock prayer meeting was one of the most precious hours I have enjoyed for a

long time. God came with power into my soul.
Salvation came in streams of light and joy. I was
made to say, "the fullness of God."

Sunday was a day long to be remembered. The
nine o'clock prayer meeting was an occasion of
power. When the invitation was given to stand up
for Jesus, as one after another rose up to bear testimony to His love and mercy, my soul was filled with
love and joy. At 11 o'clock I preached from John
3:16, with comfort, I trust, to some, and joy to my
own heart. Again at night, to a very large congregation, on the effects of sin, temporal, spiritual and
eternal. I trust some good was done.

Monday. This was the day set apart to decorate
the poor soldiers' graves. I had forgot, and an-
nounced a prayer meeting to come off at the hour,
and after I had made the appointment I felt bound to
attend. God manifested Himself to us in great
power. At the service at night two souls were
brightly converted, and one sister that had been
praying all the meeting for a new heart was made to
feel that her prayers had been heard. Thirty-five
have joined in all up to date. Oh! how meager is
one's faith!

HOLINESS CONVENTIONS.

It is peculiarly fitting that a word should be said about these religious gatherings in Georgia in the years that are gone, for one of the leading spirits in them was W. A. Dodge, who had as much to do with organizing the "Georgia Holiness Association" and with holding "Holiness Conventions" as any other advocate of sanctification in this section.

This "Association" was simply a company of people, either in the experience of perfect love, or seeking the same, all of them believing in the Wesleyan statement of the doctrine of entire sanctification, banded together for a common purpose, whose main object was to hold meetings for the promotion of this rich experience. The "Conventions," therefore, were not gatherings for the transaction of business matters, for little or nothing was done on that line, but purely to preach definitely the doctrine and urge the experience upon believers, as well as to seek the salvation of sinners. Many are living to-day who are the religious products of these soul-refreshing meetings. Really, the "Indian Springs Campground" was born in these "Conventions."

Only those who were privileged to attend them can form any correct idea of what seasons of grace they were, and what wonderful spiritual power attended them. Remarkable scenes were often witnessed, and wonderful things frequently occurred. Even the singing itself was soul-stirring, the volume of song and the heartiness of it being prominent features. These were glorious occasions, drawing together from far and near not only believers in and professors of this high grace, but attracting many spiritually-minded persons who did not see this doctrine in the same light as did these "Holiness people." At one of them, held in Warrenton, Ga., in 1884, Bishop Pierce, who did not accept the "second blessing" theory, was present, and preached with unusual power, the Holy Spirit being graciously manifest. A young man was converted and ran up into the pulpit and gathered the Bishop in his arms, rejoicing aloud. Eternity alone will reveal what was done at these "Holiness Conventions," in which W. A. Dodge took such a leading part.

These things are mentioned in order that what follows about the organization of the "Georgia Holiness Association" may be the better understood.

ORGANIZATION OF THE "GEORGIA HOLINESS ASSOCIATION" IN 1883.

The Holiness Convention held its business meeting at the house of Rev. A. J. Jarrell, in Gainesville, Ga., May 17, 1883.

President A. J. Jarrell was called to the chair.

W. A. Dodge was elected Secretary pro tem.

Present: C. A. Jamison, Milton Harris, Miller Willis, W. O. Butler, B. E. L. Timmons, J. H. Little, S. D. Evans, William Pennington, E. G. Murrah, Brother Mealy, W. C. Dunlap, W. C. Davis, A. J. Jarrell, W. A. Dodge, Geo. D. Watson.

Opened with prayer by Brother W. C. Dunlap for Divine guidance.

After prayer, Rev. Geo. D. Watson, of Newport, Ky., gave an account of similar organizations over the land. They were associations of brethren and sisters in the enjoyment of the blessing (without any constitution or by-laws), banded together to spread the doctrine and experience of holiness throughout the churches in the land. The roll is annually corrected.

FIRST RESOLUTION.

Resolved, That we, the friends of Scriptural Holiness, organize ourselves into an association, to be known as the "Georgia Holiness Association," for the spread of Scriptural Holiness throughout the churches of our State, and that we cordially invite all persons in the enjoyment, and all those who are thirsting for the experience, to unite with us in the work, and to enroll their names as such, and to pray for each other.

This was carried unanimously.

The following names were enrolled. (See list below.)

SECOND RESOLUTION.

Resolved, That the officers of the association or convention consist of a president, two vice-presidents, secretary and treasurer, the last two to be combined in the same person.

The convention then went into the election of officers.

A. J. Jarrell, President, Gainesville, Ga.

B. F. Farris, 1st Vice-President, West Point, Ga.

G. H. Patillo, 2d Vice-President, Griffin, Ga.

W. A. Dodge, Secretary and Treasurer, Atlanta, Ga.

These to hold for one year, or until their successors are elected.

THIRD RESOLUTION.

Resolved, That the Convention elect annually an executive committee of five, consisting of the officers of the Association, and one additional. Adopted.

EXECUTIVE COMMITTEE.

Rev. A. J. Jarrell, Gainesville, Ga., chairman; Rev. B. F. Farris, West Point, Ga.; Rev. G. H. Patillo, Griffin, Ga.; Rev. W. A. Dodge, Atlanta, Ga.; Rev. W. C. Davis, Macon, Ga.

FOURTH RESOLUTION.

Resolved, That the Convention adopt "The Way of Life," edited and published in Atlanta, Ga., by Rev. W. A. Dodge, as the organ of the Association, and that we work for it. Carried.

FIFTH RESOLUTION.

Resolved, That we hold in Autumn of this year another Holiness Convention or camp-meeting. Time and place to be arranged by the Executive Committee. Carried.

The Convention then adjourned *sine die.*

A. J. JARRELL, *President.*

W. A. DODGE, *Secretary.*

ROLL, MAY 17, 1883.

Rev. A. J. Jarrell, Gainesville, Ga.
Rev. C. A. Jamison, Clayton, Ga.
Milton Harris, Eudora, Ga.
S. M. Willis, Charleston, S. C.
Rev. W. O. Butler, Carnesville, Ga.
Rev. B. E. L. Timmons, Calhoun, Ga.
Mrs. Lucy C. H. Timmons, Calhoun, Ga.
Rev. John H. Little, Dawsonville, Ga.
Mrs. Neppie J. Little, Dawsonville, Ga.
Rev. Wm. A. Parks, Whitesburg, Ga.
Rev. S. D. Evans, Clayton, Ga.
Rev. B. F. Farris, West Point, Ga.
J. M. Venable, Louisville, Ga.
Rev. E. G. Murrah, Winterville, Ga.
W. B. R. Pennington, Pennington, Ga.
Geo. Mealy.
Rev. W. C. Dunlap, Jonesboro, Ga.
Rev. Geo. D. Watson, Newport, Ky.
Rev. W. C. Davis, Macon, Ga.
T. A. Daniel.
Jas. T. Vaughn, Harmony Grove, Ga.
Rev. E. M. Stanton, Adairsville, Ga.
Emma J. Barr, Edgefield C. H., S. C.
Mrs. H. N. Ware, Gainesville, Ga.
Miss Dora Rakestraw, Gainesville, Ga.
Henry B. Hearn, Eatonton, Ga.
Mrs. R. C. Hargrove, Gainesville, Ga.
R. C. Maddox, Gainesville, Ga.

Robt. H. Stancill, Gainesville, Ga.

Mrs. M. J. Mosley, Pennington, Ga.

Mrs. Parmelia Alman, Atlanta, Ga.

Rev. W. A. Dodge, Atlanta, Ga.

Mrs. A. Roberts, Conyers, Ga.

Rev. H. M. Newton, Lawrenceville, Ga.

Rev. C. C. Cary, Thomson, Ga.

D. F. Irving, Thomson, Ga.

Rev. J. W. Cook, Eudora, Ga.

Rev. J. A. Turner, Eudora, Ga.

R. H. Smith, Gainesville, Ga.

M. S. Seymour, Gainesville, Ga.

J. W. Leach, Gainesville, Ga.

Mrs. Mary Leach, Gainesville, Ga.

A. C. Doster.

Mrs. Breeland Harris.

Mrs. P. T. Collier, Blue Springs, Ga.

Mrs. Hester M. Marrow, Senoia, Ga.

Willie Sutton.

Rev. Geo. W. Duval, Warrenton, Ga.

Rev. Uriah Langford, Warrenton, Ga.

Rev. T. H. Hunnicutt, Red Hill, Ga.

Rev. J. P. Ledbetter, Red Hill, Ga.

J. C. Akins, Red Hill, Ga.

Mrs. N. C. Shannon, Red Hill, Ga.

Mrs. Mary Davis, Red Hill, Ga.

J. A. Hall.

Mrs. J. A. Hall, Red Hill, Ga.

D. C. Crenshaw, Red Hill, Ga.

Mrs. Martha James, Cromer's Mill, Ga.

Mrs. C. H. Fowler, Cromer's Mill, Ga.

Mrs. Tabitha Smith, Cromer's Mill, Ga.

Rev. J. O. Varner, Bold Springs, Ga.

Jas. M. Moore, Bold Springs, Ga.

Wm. T. Jackson, Culverton, Ga.

Isabella Jackson, Culverton, Ga.

Thomas J. Waller, Culverton, Ga.

John M. Jackson, Culverton, Ga.

Jas. T. Burnley, Powellton, Ga.

John W. Waller, Powellton. Ga.

Johnnie Shields, Powellton, Ga.

C. E. Little, Milledgeville, Ga.

Henry F. Russell, Augusta, Ga.

F. A. Hall, Milledgeville, Ga.

John H. Curry, Macon, Ga.

John W. Wallace, Augusta, Ga.

Mrs. Amelia Sexton, Clanton, Ala.

Mrs. Lula Dudley, Lomax, Ala.

Mrs. L. A. Coachman, Camilla, Ga.

Mrs. Nancy Aikens, Crane Eater, Ga.

Mrs. H. A. Morrow, Sonora, Ga.

Rev. T. A. Seals, Marietta, Ga.

Mrs. S. A. Fite, Gainesville, Ga.

Mrs. S. E. Carpenter, Blackshear, Ga.

J. M. Johnson, Eatonton, Ga.

Rev. S. P. Owens, Shadydale, Ga.

Rev. R. C. Oliver, Spartanburg, S. C.

J. R. Harwell, West Point, Ga.

Mrs. P. A. Schenk, Atlanta, Ga.

Mrs. Elizabeth E. Martin, Atlanta, Ga.

Mrs. W. H. Anderson, Brunswick, Ga.

Mrs. Camilla L. Almand, Atlanta, Ga.

Miss Elizabeth J. White, Ophir, Ga.

Mrs. N. J. Daniel, Thomson, Ga.

F. M. Stubbs, Augusta, Ga.

D. M. Crawford, Macon, Ga.

Thos. B. Young, Thomson, Ga.

Mrs. S. J. Young, Thomson, Ga.

Mrs. S. H. Reese, Thomson, Ga.

M. C. Fulton, Thomson, Ga.

Rev. J. N. Myers, Banksville, Ga.

R. B. Morris, Augusta, Ga.

Mrs. Mary H. Morris, Augusta, Ga.

J. P. Bondurant, Augusta, Ga.

J. C. Sorrow, Maysville, Ga.

Mrs. Sarah E. Sorrow, Maysville, Ga.

W. E. H. Searcy, Griffin, Ga.

W. J. Deas, Augusta, Ga.

Josiah Miller, Augusta, Ga.

Armstrong Conner, Augusta, Ga.

Mrs. S. D. Wooten, Milledgeville, Ga.

Mrs. Lutecia Massy, Milledgeville, Ga.

Geo. W. Carraker, Milledgeville, Ga.

Mattie L. Hall, Milledgeville, Ga.

Matilda Mixson, Milledgeville, Ga.

Mrs. M. F. Deas, Augusta, Ga.

W. J. Deas, Augusta, Ga.

Mrs. Annie Lynch, Milledgeville, Ga.

Mrs. Martha Richards, Milledgeville, Ga.

Augustus Green, Rome, Ga.

Miss Cora Gum, Milledgeville, Ga.

Rev. J. M. Armstrong, Norwood, Ga.

Rev. Robt M. Cook, Sparta, Ga.

J. O. Clay, Akin, S. C.

John C. Ferris, Augusta, Ga.

J. E. Duren, Augusta, Ga.

G. L. Slaton, Harmony Grove, Ga.

John R. Robinson, Lawrenceville, Ga.

John M. Eldridge, Huntsville, Ala.

Rev. W. B. Godbey, Carlisle, Ky.

Rev. B. A. Johnson, Norwood, Ga.

Mrs. M. R. Johnson, Norwood, Ga.

Miss Amanda M. Johnson, Norwood, Ga.

C. R. Elliott, Macon, Ga.

W. F. Coones, Macon, Ga.

Mrs. Mary Hockinghull, Barrettsville, Ga.

Rev. R. F. Williamson, Ellaville, Ga.

Rev. J. W. Simmons, Macon, Ga.

Rev. T. T. Christian, Savannah, Ga.

Rev. T. H. Christian, Oxford, Ga.

Mrs. Lucy T. Christian, Savannah, Ga.

Miss Mary W. Christian, Savannah, Ga.

1884.

Rev. J. S. Jordan, Lumpkin, Ga.

Mrs. Eleanor Brown, Augusta, Ga.

Mrs. M. J. Sims, Augusta, Ga.

Mrs. Mary A. Barnes, Atlanta, Ga.

Rev. J. C. Edmondson, Gainesville, Ga.

Mrs. M. M. Edmondson, Gainesville, Ga.

E. C. Barrett, Gainesville, Ga.

Rev. J. W. Hargrove, Gainesville, Ga.

P. C. Williams, Gainesville, Ga.

Thos. Thrower, Atlanta, Ga.

J. W. Slocumb, Clinton, Ga.

J. A. Allen, Warrenton, Ga.

F. P. Sherman, Gainesville, Ga.

Miss Neicie Farbee, Gainesville, Ga.

Rev. C. B. Lahatte, Gainesville, Ga.

Mrs. M. E. Lahatte, Gainesville, Ga.

E. H. Seymour, Gainesville, Ga.

Mrs. Ada Seymour, Gainesville, Ga.

F. F. Wilson, Maysville, Ga.

George Rakestraw, Gainesville, Ga.

Rev. J. W. Blosser, Atlanta, Ga.

Mrs. Margaret Blosser, Atlanta, Ga.

Mrs. Nannie Rakestraw, Gainesville, Ga.

Dr. J. F. Vaughn, Harmony Grove, Ga.

Mrs. Orpha Vaughn, Harmony Grove, Ga.

W. J. Freeman, Augusta, Ga.

Mrs. Mildred A. Freeman, Augusta, Ga.

Mrs. D. C. White, Brunswick, Ga.

Jas. Bledsoe Armstrong, Norwood, Ga.

Miss M. L. Evans, Macon, Ga.

Rev. C. Pope, Augusta, Ga.

Miss Gussie Shaw, Augusta, Ga.

Miss Julia Ramsey, Augusta, Ga.

J. E. Martin, Augusta, Ga.

Mrs. Fannie M. Oliver, Spartanburg, S. C.

Rev. R. C. Oliver, Spartanburg, S. C.

Thos. P. Reynolds, Augusta, Ga.

Mrs. M. E. Walker, Augusta, Ga.

Rev. J. E. Evans, Macon, Ga.

W. A. Deas, Augusta, Ga.

R. H. Hill, Augusta, Ga.

9 d

"THIS NIGHT THY SOUL SHALL BE REQUIRED OF THEE."

It was at camp-meeting in a Western State, about 1894, at the last service, when there came a fearful rain storm, accompanied with vivid lightning and loud peals of thunder. The sound of the rain on the roof of the stand made so much noise that nothing could be done but sing, and thus the time was spent. About 9 o'clock there was a lull in the storm, and Rev. W. A. Dodge was asked to speak to the people, when he arose, and earnestly urged all who were unsaved to immediately seek salvation, and then invited sinners to the altar. A few responded, and the invitation was continued.

Just about that moment there came a very vivid flash of lightning, accompanied by the immediate crash of thunder, for a bolt had struck just outside the graveyard fence near the stand. Fear was in the hearts of many, and then sinners began to rush to the altar without much persuasion. It was soon filled with serious souls inquiring the way of salvation, and very soon several were converted.

During this service Brother Dodge, as usual in such meetings, was quite active in the congregation in endeavoring to persuade sinners to give their hearts to God, and in the altar in instructing penitents what they must do to be saved.

The meeting closed, and the people left the stand. Two young ladies were in the congregation, but had not yielded to the appeals which had been made. They started home, and had to cross a stream, greatly swollen by the heavy rain. Unfortunately, the team was swept down by the swift moving current, and both girls met a watery grave. Not until next morning were their bodies found. The occurrence cast a deep gloom upon the surrounding country. After earnest searching, the dead forms of these bright girls were discovered just below the ford entangled in the bushes.

Before leaving the camp-ground for home, Brother Dodge went where the bodies were laid out, and one of the faces he recognized as that of a young woman with whom he had talked the night before about her soul, whom he had urged to seek religion, and whom he had faithfully warned. Neither one of the girls were religious. That night's service at the camp-meeting was their last opportunity to be saved, and Rev. W. A. Dodge was the last one to warn them of their danger.

TWO INCIDENTS.

Those who looked upon Brother Dodge's face and noted his sweetness of spirit, being always so cheerful, never knew the sore trials of the inner man. He was not exempted from those peculiar temptations which belong to the life of an itinerant preacher. He knew what sore trials were, though he never talked about them, nor showed the effect of them in his face or spirit. He could be as firm as any other man when duty demanded it, and never shrunk from declaring himself against sin when occasion seemed to require it. The quiet, sweet-spirited man could be as bold as a lion, and firm as adamant, when duty called him to the front.

While he was pastor in Gainesville, whiskey was sold in the county. In his pulpit ministrations and in his intercourse with neighbors and friends, he never failed to bear open testimony against this great evil.

One Sabbath his soul was moved within him, and he declared with emphasis that as much liquor was sold in drug-stores in Gainesville on Sunday as in saloons in one day of the week. The shot hit the mark, and created a stir. A druggist in town became greatly offended, and started an effort to have Brother Dodge removed at the next Conference, securing the names of nine persons to the petition. How far they succeeded it is not now necessary to know. Enough to say this man of God heard of it, and it hurt him to the quick. But he swerved not one inch from the right because of the opposition.

Brother Dodge went down about Barnesville, Ga., to assist in a meeting, for he knew not how to refuse the appeals of the brethren. How he did revel in revival services, especially when sinners were seeking the Lord!

He was at home under such surroundings, and was a perfect general in an altar service. On this occasion a Dutchman chanced to come to the services, a regular beer-drinker, and conviction seized him. After a season he was graciously converted. At an experience meeting held later he arose to tell what the Lord had done for him. He was large and stout, just about the figure of our departed brother. Standing a moment, the Dutchman began to talk after this fashion:

"My friends (stroking himself in front a moment), I used to take a drink of peer after breakfast, and it make me feel goot down here. Den at dinner time I take anodder glass of peer, and it make me feel goot. Den at night I takes anodder glass of peer, and I feels goot. But der come dis man Dodge down here, and he talk about one named Jesus, who he say could save men from sins. I believe in Jesus, and He saves me. And I got Him now in my heart right here (putting his hand upon his breast), and I feel mighty goot."

One can almost see the smile playing over the face of Brother Dodge as he looked at, and listened to this simple-minded foreigner while he was telling his experience in his own way.

PREACHING AT CONFERENCE.

Not often was this itinerant preacher put up to preach when he went to Conference, but at the session of the North Georgia Conference, held at Trinity Church, Atlanta, Ga., in November, 1900, he was appointed to preach on Saturday night, not a good night as all know, for a congregation, since even preachers take the liberty on that night to remain away from public service.

He had a small crowd, but it affected him very little. Taking as his text James 1 : 17 : "Every good gift and every perfect gift is from above, and cometh down from the Father of lights, with whom is no variableness, neither shadow of turning," he explained each phrase, and threw a flood of light on the text.

Coming out of the church, Rev. Felix P. Brown, now a superannuated preacher, a good judge of preaching, said to a brother preacher: "Clem, they ought to make Asbury Dodge preach to the North Georgia Conference every year." And this good brother was not far wrong.

A LETTER OF REV. W. A. DODGE.

If we would get a clear view of one's inner character, it is well to read his letters. Here is one showing the spirit of this good man, and his very humble opinion of himself. Some dissatisfaction had been expressed at a matter with which he was connected by those in church authority, for which Brother Dodge was not to blame, and this letter has to do with that incident.

ATLANTA, GA., March 12, 1903.

MY DEAR CLEM: Yours, with communication from ————, received. I am sorry to have been the occasion of this delay and dissatisfaction to the management. I rather think, as the matter stands, I had better resign and let some one else be put in my place who will give satisfaction.

What do you think? Of course I am willing to do my part in these things, but when I try and fail, and there are so many others who can do better than I can, I am embarrassed to try to fill a place for which it seems I am incompetent. Be honest and frank with me, and speak out your mind. I can drop out at next Conference, and another can take my place.

God bless you and yours. Pray for me.

Lovingly, yours in Jesus,

W. A. DODGE.

THE DEATH OF HIS MOTHER.

No man loved his mother more than W. A. Dodge. In this respect he was a true son, whose heart always beat loyally to her who gave him being, and whose early efforts made the first good impressions on his mind and gave the right turn to his life. Among his "sketches," hid away, was found this notice of his mother, for it seemed he wanted to lay it up among his treasures:

(From *Macon (Ga.) Telegraph.*)

Mrs. I. C. Dodge Passes Away.

Died Yesterday Afternoon from Old Age—Funeral to Occur this Morning from the Residence.

Mrs. I. C. Dodge died yesterday afternoon at 6 o'clock at her residence on Huguenin Heights, Macon, Ga., from old age. Mrs. Dodge was seventy-eight years of age, and had been in feeble health for some time.

Mrs. Dodge was formerly of Columbia county, and has a large circle of friends in Macon, who will be pained to hear of her death. She leaves one son, Rev. Mr. Dodge, of Atlanta, also, a granddaughter, Mrs. C. D. Peavey, of Macon. Mrs. J. D. Bowles, of Macon, was a daughter of Mrs. Dodge.

The funeral will take place this morning from the residence of Mrs. J. D. Bowles at 7:30 o'clock. The remains will leave for Harlem, Ga., at nine o'clock. The funeral services will be conducted by Revs. Bardwell and Harrison.

The interment will be in Mercer cemetery, near Harlem.

A LOOK INTO HIS "SKETCHES OF SERMONS."

This side of our brother's character is worthy of study, and brings up many interesting things. He was unique in his make-up, and was unlike any other preacher in the type of his mind, in the manner of dividing his texts, and in his delivery. He had a systematic and analytical mind, and hence he always divided his subjects into several heads. He was never afraid of "firstly, secondly, thirdly," etc., for he often went up to "eighthly." The joints of his sermons could be plainly seen, for they were anything else than essays, or compositions, with no divisions, and nothing to separate the different points made.

He rarely wrote a sermon out in full, always made notes, and his "sketches and skeletons," which he left in systematic order, are numbered by the hundreds. He had a "letter and invoice file," large and well filled with these "Sketches," and they reveal the mind of this devoted man and faithful preacher. If any one supposes he confined himself alone in his preaching to the doctrine of "sanctification," he will find himself very much mistaken. These "sketches" embrace almost every conceivable Bible subject, for W. A. Dodge was essentially and pre-eminently a Bible preacher. He held himself exclusively to scriptural subjects, and had neither time nor disposition to treat of novel ideas or curious questions,

which have such great attraction for some ministers
in these modern times.

It was necessary with his peculiar type of mind to
make notes, and these he used freely.   In fact he
rarely ever preached without "notes."   In this way
he prepared his sermons.   He carefully divided the
text and subject in a very simple and intelligent way,
and held his mind down to it, using illustrations from
Scripture, as well as drawing upon every outside
source for material to throw light upon his subject
and to enforce the truth he was seeking to present.
In his "sketches" are found some he borrowed from
others, for he seemed not to care especially for novelty or originality in selecting divisions of a text.
If he found something in a paper, or read a sermon
which divided itself suitable to his notions, he ap-
propriated it, using his own words and ideas to fill
out the sermon.

In one case, in his early ministry, he borrowed the
divisions of Mr. Wesley on "Salvation by Faith,"
from the text, "By grace are ye saved by faith,"
which he used effectively.

On the back of this "sketch" just mentioned are
these words: "Written at Camp No. 3, James Island,
S. C., January 25, 1864," showing that it was while
he was a young preacher and chaplain in the army,
and doubtless it was preached to the Confederate soldiers at that place.

How this carries the mind back to those dark days
of the civil war, forty-three years ago!   How many
things come up in imagination as we think of this

almost beardless boy standing up among these men in grey, preaching to them salvation from sin by faith in Christ here and now! the same Gospel, however, he preached to the end of his long and useful life.

Here is another "sketch," made about the same time on James Island, in 1864. It seems to be on the "deceitfulness of sin:"

Text—"But exhort one another daily, while it is called to-day, lest any of you be hardened through the deceitfulness of sin."

1st. Sin is the same the world over. 2d. The motives we have. 3d. We try to cover our sins. 4th. We hunt pleasure in sin. 5th. We think we can satisfy ourselves in sin. 6th. Sin deceives us into procrastination. 7th. How can we love sin like we do?

He seemed to have changed his base some time in 1864, for here is a "sketch" with this written on the back: "Written March 24, 1864, at Camp Milton, Fla."

Just above it are these words: "Preached at or in 23d Georgia regiment, March 26, 1864." Here is the "sketch:"

Habbakkuk, 3:2d verse: "O Lord, revive Thy work in the midst of the years; in the midst of the years make known. In wrath remember mercy."

These were the words of this man of God, as he lamented over the sinful condition of this people.

I. We will notice:

1st. Their sinfulness.

2d. Their danger of a disgracful overthrow.

II. The reasons for their imminent danger was:

1st. Because they had forgotten God.

2d. And because they would not return.

III. Then let us compare ourselves with this wicked nation:

1st. We have sinned as a nation and as individuals.

2d. Our danger as a nation and as individuals.

IV. The reasons of our troubles and now impending destruction are:

1st. We have forgotten God.

2d. And we do not turn as we should.

3d. Then let us view it like this man of God, and work and pray like he did.

Possibly one of the most interesting sketches of that period long past, is one he made on the back of a request to the captain commanding to be allowed to visit Charleston, S. C., while he was in camp at James Island. Here is the written request:

CAMP 23D GA. REGIMENT,
James Island, S. C., December 23, 1863.

"Captain—

"SIR: I respectfully ask leave of Gen'l Colquitt to visit the city of Charleston, and to return to camp at pleasure, for the next thirty days.

"Very respectfully, etc.,

"W. A. DODGE,

"Chaplain 23d Ga. Reg't."

"To Captain George G. Gratin,

"Adjutant."

The sermon appears to have been on "God and His Attributes," and this is the sketch. He fails to give the text used on this occasion:

Unity—one God. Eternity—from everlasting. Spirituality—not body or matter. Omniscence—He knoweth all things. Omnipotence—He hath all power. Omnipresence—His care over us. Immutability—He never changeth. Goodness—He is always kind. Mercy—He dealeth mercifully. Justice —and yet He is just. Truth—He is ever truthful.

Consider then:

Is He not a God worthy of our most humble homage? Where can we find any one whose attributes are equal to His? Look around you and try, and see if you can find anything which can cope with Him? I wish you to examine His attributes, compare them with yourselves, and then see if you are not an object of minor importance. Let us then worship and adore His great and Exalted Personage.

On the back of the "sketch" are these notes: "Written at Camp No. 2, James Island, S. C., November 7, 1863. Where and when preached—March 26th, 1864, 27th Georgia Regiment. October —, 1863, 23d Georgia Regiment."

We can almost see this young preacher, just starting out on a long life and a useful course, as he stood up among those hardy soldiers in grey, speaking to them of God, and urging them to serve, to worship and adore Him. It may not have been a sermon after the fashion of some we hear from educated men, but it had in it scriptural truth, and came from a heart all on fire for God and with the love of souls therein.

There are other "sketches" preserved from those fearful war times, on faded paper, written with pen and ink. One of these is on John 15:25: "They hated me without a cause." And on the back is the usual note: "Written at Camp No. 3, James Island, S. C., January 25th, 1864." Then follow the words: "Where preached"—the date not being filled out, indicating that he forgot to make a note of when it was preached.

Another "sketch" of those war days is on Acts, 16:30, 31: "Sirs, what must I do to be saved? And they said, Believe on the Lord Jesus Christ, and thou shalt be saved and thy house."

This has on the back the same note as the foregoing, showing it was made out on January 25, 1864, while in camp on James Island, S. C. It is not stated when and where it was preached.

Coming down later, we find a multitude of subjects upon which he preached. He neglected no important doctrine or duty in God's Word. He believed in the "tithe rule" of giving, conscientiously setting aside one-tenth of all he received from God, and so it is no surprise that we find some "sketches" on "giving," and one or two on "tithing." In this matter, as in all others, W. A. Dodge invariably practiced what he preached. He never urged upon others what he did not either do himself, or endeavor to do.

Here is a sketch on "Different Kinds of Prayer,"

from the text, 1 Timothy, 2:1, in which the several kinds of prayer are named, "supplications, intercessions, thanksgiving." Then follow "objects of prayer," and the "things to pray for," with the closing point, "such living and praying is pleasing to God our Saviour."

Another is on "the Bible," in which he endeavors to show it is inspired, teaches of Christ, can be understood, we ought to know it, we must search it, it is for our learning and our admonition, each point fortified by a passage from the Scriptures, for he was nothing if not a scriptural preacher. He was absolutely shut up to the Word of God in searching for text and subject as well as proofs.

He was a strong believer in total abstinence, and practiced it. Here is a "sketch" on indulgence in strong drink. He states what he terms "Self-evident propositions on the subject of temperance," which are as follows:

1. No man has a right to do anything that will injure his health.

2. No man has a right to do anything which will injure his religious experience.

3. No man has a right to do anything as an example, which, if followed by others, will injure them.

4. No man has a right to place himself in the way of temptation to sin.

5. No Christian has the right to do anything that has the appearance of evil in it.

A companion sketch to the foregoing is one on

"Reasons for Prohibition," in which twelve reasons are named:

1. Rum deprives men of their reason for the time being.

2. Rum destroys men of the greatest intellectual strength.

3. Rum fosters and encourages every species of immorality.

4. Rum causes an immense expense to prevent crime.

5. Rum burdens the country with enormous taxes.

6. Rum bars the progress of civilization and religion.

7. Rum prevents reformation.

8. Rum causes the majority of the cases of insanity.

9. Rum destroys the peace of hundreds of thousands of families.

10. Rum burdens sober people for the support of paupers.

11. Its use is contrary to the Bible and common sense.

12. We have a right to rid ourselves of the burden.

Space is too limited to go much farther into these "sketches," but mention may be made of those on "The Sabbath," "On the Danger of Riches," on "The Christian Citizen in his Relations," on "Four Agents in Salvation—the Word, the Blood, the Holy Spirit, and Faith, the Appropriating Agent."

Another we find on "Seeking the Lord," from Isaiah, 55:5, 6, in which he answers three questions:

"Why seek the Lord? For what seek the Lord? How seek the Lord? When seek the Lord?" We find one on "The Sum of all Religion," from Timothy, I:5: "The end of the commandment is love out of a pure heart."

It may be truthfully said, that if these sketches were put in pamphlet form, they would be very serviceable to young preachers in giving them needful information as to how to divide texts intelligently, and how to make their points clear and forceful. They are very suggestive to a thoughful, studious preacher.

In Brother Dodge's preaching there was nothing muddy or confusing.

You could always clearly understand at what he was driving, whether you agreed with him or not, for his mind was invariably clear, and in this he is worthy to be patterned after by young preachers. "Sketches and skeletons" are sometimes tabooed, but they are invaluable to those just starting to preach in teaching them many things in treating a text of which they are ignorant.

He was always on the watch for a subject on which to preach, often catching up the divisions of others on texts and subjects. So we find clippings from papers and tracts, containing "sketches" which seemed to strike his fancy, and he laid them aside for future use. All sorts and sizes of paper are used in these "sketches" which he made, for whenever anything occurred to him, no matter where he was, he noted it down at once, not trusting to memory.

So we find several "sketches" on old bill heads of
"The Way of Life," some on note paper, others on
all sizes of scraps of paper. He was indeed a "work-
man needing not to be ashamed," for it was peculiarly true of him—he studied "to show himself ap-
proved of God," and applied himself in order to be
pre-eminently *a preacher*, for a preacher of the Word
he was. No man who knew W. A. Dodge will ever
doubt that statement.

What a history would these "sketches" reveal if
we could go back over the ground where the sermons were delivered! Preached as they were in
many States, and on numberless occasions, how
many thousands must have been touched by them
as this faithful watchman on the walls blew the
warning trumpet, or, as the Lord's messenger, he
delivered God's message to saint and sinner! Who
can calculate what these many "sketches" will mean
in the characters formed, hearts touched, lives
blessed, and souls saved? How memory loves to
play about this thought! But only the revelations
of the judgment day will fully discover all that was
accomplished by these sermons preached on so many
different occasions.

This "file" of "sketches" give us some idea of the
ammunition which this faithful soldier of the cross
used in combating the devil and fighting the foes of
God and man. These were Brother Dodge's materials for preaching, that responsible task imposed
upon him by the Holy Ghost, and which was to him
the joy of his heart. Doubtless whenever he took

a trip off, the "file" accompanied him. They represented the results of his preparations and study for years. In this he was a wise preacher. He saved the materials of a sermon, for he had no false pride nor ambition for novelty. When occasion demanded it, he preached the same sermon again. So we will find among these "sketches" duplicates, which clearly indicate he sometimes repeated sermons preached elsewhere.

For instance, here is one on "Quench not the Spirit," 1st Thessalonians, 5:19, preached, written November 11, 1865, and he preached it again in 1868.

It would be intensely interesting to go further into these "sketches," but space forbids. The more we examine them, the more we see the infinite variety of subjects upon which this efficient, well-qualified, and faithful man preached. Quite every one is on some practical line, for he had no time to waste on visionary or sentimental themes. How many souls were converted, instructed or helped under these sermons, heaven only knows.

A sketch which deserves particular mention, since he had a great fight during his pastorate while in Eatonton, Ga., on the question of which this treats, is on "Dancing," in which he exhaustively treats the subject. It is worth while to have that "sketch" printed and read by thousands, since it is thorough, clear, pointed, reasonable and scriptural.

CLEMENT C. CARY,
Gainesville, Ga.

"THE DOUBLE-MINDED."

W. A. DODGE, ATLANTA, GA.

"A double-minded man is unstable in all his ways" (James 1 : 8).

There are but two minds in the world,—one is the mind of Christ, the other of Satan. Sinners have but the evil, while the fully saved have only the mind of Christ. And yet St. James tells us that there is a "double-minded man." The true meaning of the text is looking two ways. One looks forward, the other backward. Christ said: "No man, having put his hand to the plough, and looking back, is fit for the kingdom of God" (Luke 9 : 62).

The mind of Christ looks forward, while the mind of Satan looks backward. God put his seal of condemnation on this looking-back mind in his command and dealing with Lot's wife. The angel said, "Escape for thy life; look not behind thee" (Gen. 19 : 17). In going out, Lot's wife, not forgetting, but remembering the things left behind, turned and looked back, and she became a pillar of salt (Gen. 19 : 26).

Paul in telling his experience uses this very same figure. In his letter to the church at Philippi, when telling them that he had given up all for Christ, that he might attain unto the resurrection of the dead, he says that in the sense of the glorified resurrected

state he had not attained, then adds, "This one thing
I do, forgetting those things which are behind, and
reaching forth unto those things which are before, I
press toward the mark for the prize of the high calling of God in Christ Jesus. Let us, therefore, as
many as be perfect, be thus minded." (Phil. 3 : 13-
15). He plainly shows that only the sanctified have
the one mind that looks forward. The statement of
our Lord, that while the man had taken the gospel
plow, he was looking back, shows he had yet something in him that made him look back and that needed to be cleansed away, in order to have but the one
mind that looks forward.

St. James says that this double mind makes the
possessor vacillating. The civil war within the soul
carries first one way and then the other. One mind
says, "Read the Bible." The other says, "Read the
newspapers." One says, "Go to church." The other
says, "Stay at home." One says "Hold family
prayer," while the other says, "Go to bed." One
says, "Support the gospel." The other says, "Look
out for number one." This accounts for the irregu-
larities in the lives of thousands of people that profess religion. To an interested observer this is one
of the most painful of subjects to contemplate.

It is a sad fact that not one in a hundred who fails
to go forward and obtain deliverance from the double mind, stands firm in his Christian experience.

Backsliding begins always first in the heart before
it is manifest in the life. Thousands are conscious
of a decline in their heart life who never show it in

their outer conduct. Loss of the fruits of the Spirit or declining in them is heart experience in backsliding. All that we ever found who were never conscious of a decline at some time in their Christian life, have belonged to that company known as the entirely sanctified, who subsequently to their conversion, obtained the blessing of entire sanctification.

I. There are other results that come because of the presence of the double mind. This is demonstrated by the apostle in this epistle. Indeed, it seems to us that he wrote the letter to lead the Christians to whom he addressed it into the experience of heart cleansing. This is the golden thread that runs through all the apostolic letters, and in fact the whole Bible.

1. The "fleshly mind" of Satan makes us to repine at trials.

We are exhorted by the apostle James (1:2): "My brethren, count it all joy when ye fall into divers temptations." The expression "divers temptations" means testing of all kinds. But instead of rejoicing, the carnal mind takes to murmuring at them. Testings are needful experiences. They reveal what is, and what is not in the heart. We have eye tests, muscle tests, ear tests, and shall we not have spiritual tests? A test of faith on a plain "Thus saith the Lord" demonstrates to us whether there is doubt lingering in the heart or not. A test of love reveals to us the presence or absence of temper; of humility, whether there is any pride lingering in the soul; of liberality, if there be any covetousness remaining; of submission, whether rebellion is to be found asserting itself or not. When testings come on these or any other lines, and we find the two opposite principles contending within, it should be taken as conclusive proof of the double mind remaining.

2. The "fleshly mind" makes us weak in the presence of temptation. "Blessed is the man that endureth temptation. . . . . Every man is tempted, when he is drawn away of his own lust, and enticed" (James 1:12, 14).

There is no sin in temptation. If there is, Jesus our Lord was a great sinner, and the Holy Ghost was accessory. He was "tempted in all points like as we are, yet without sin," and the Holy Ghost led Him up into the wilderness to be tempted of the devil. As long as the double mind remains, there is danger of yielding. The Master said, "The prince of this world [Satan] cometh and findeth nothing in me." No double mind, hence no disposition within to yield to the suggestion of evil from without. No lust to draw Him away and entice. God has promised that we shall not be tempted beyond that we are able to bear. By the mouth of the apostle James he announces, "Blessed is the man that endureth temptation."

It is charged by some that the sanctified claim freedom from temptation. This is one of the tricks of the enemy. Of all people they are the ones upon whom Satan tries his skill most ingeniously and persistently.

Freedom from temptation is proof conclusive that we do not belong to even the justified, for why should Satan trouble himself about those who are his already?

An infidel master berated his Christian servant for complaining at his tribulations and trials, saying, "You a Christian and have so many conflicts. I am not a professor of religion, but do not have any of the things to trouble me of which you complain." The servant could not answer, until one day while out hunting, and the master had fired into a flock of wild ducks, killing one and wounding another. The master cried out, "Run, Charley, run, don't let him get away." The faithful servant soon returned bearing the wounded duck in his hand, saying, "Massa, I see how it is now. You say you has no trials, tribulations, and I has dem. It's 'cause you is de debil's dead duck, while I is de Lord's lame duck, and de debil he all de time try ketch me."

If you want all the black ranks of darkness turned loose on you, get the blessing of entire sanctification. If you want to get where you can meet these legions of the pit, though hoofed and horned, marching in solid phalanx against you, and be enabled to stand against all their fiery darts, get the blessing of full salvation. To all such the divine pledge is given, "As thy days so shall thy strength be."

3. This double-mindedness makes us respecters of persons. "If there come into your assembly a man with a gold ring, in goodly apparel, and there come in also a poor man in vile raiment; and ye have

respect to him that weareth the gay clothing, and say unto him, Sit thou here in a good place; and say to the poor, Stand thou there, or sit here under my footstool: are ye not then partial in yourselves, and have become judges of evil thoughts?"

Alas! who has not seen this many times repeated? This mixed state makes our love heterogenous, *i. e.,* to love those who think, feel, talk, and act as we do; while the sanctified mind alone makes our love homogeneous, *i. e.* God-like, loving all men alike, whether good, bad, or indifferent. God loved and gave His Son to die for an African or Chinaman, as well as an Anglo-Saxon. The sanctified heart can put the arms of its faith and love about the lowest and meanest of Adam's race, as well as the best. The want of this state makes thousands shun the slums and with folded skirts to walk by the fallen in the ditch.

The double mind makes one talk two ways. "Out of the same mouth proceedeth blessing and cursing [or scolding]. My brethren, these things ought not so to be. Doth a fountain send forth at the same place sweet water and bitter?" (James 3: 10, 11). The word "curse" should be rendered "scold," for Christian people do not swear, but how often do we find them to be regular old scolds? Mr. Wesley said that he would no more fret and worry than he would curse and swear. A sanctified heart has a sanctified conversation and a sanctified tone in the voice. St. James says such is "not from above, but is earthly, sensual, devilish;" while the conversation that is born of the heavenly mind is "pure, peace-

able, gentle, easy to be entreated, full of mercy and
good fruits, without partiality and without hypocrisy." To the face, the double-minded will frequently use flattery, while behind the back they will find
fault. While the heart is double, with only one
tongue with which to talk, the conversation will be
double, for these two opposite minds can not talk
the same way. These things ought not so to be, and
they are not in nature, but, alas! it is so with the
double-minded.

The difficulty is not with the tongue, but is farther
back and deeper down. "Out of the heart proceed
evil thoughts," etc. "Out of the abundance of the
heart, the mouth speaketh." "As a man thinketh in
his heart, so is he." It is not the stream that needs
to be purified, but the fountain. A sanctified heart
will have a sanctified conversation.

4. The double mind produces inward conflicts.

"From whence come wars and fightings among
[or within] you? Come they not hence, even of
your lusts that war in your members?" (James
4:1).

Paul, in Galatians 5:17, says: "For the flesh lust-
eth against the Spirit, and the Spirit against the
flesh: and these are contrary, the one to the other:
so that ye can not do the things that ye would."
Who can describe the unceasing conflict that goes
on day and night in the heart of the double-minded?
No language can portray it. Day and night the battle rages. And if at any time the hostilities seem to
cease, and the conclusion is reached that the civil

war within is at an end, never to be resumed, how soon it is discovered to be only a temporary suspension, in order to open again on some new line! When these battles are renewed from time to time, the cry is often extorted, as from Paul, "O wretched man that I am! who shall deliver me from the body of this death" (Rom. 7:24),—but these persons fail to go over into the experience of the next verse. which exultantly exclaims, "I thank God through Jesus Christ our Lord."

The blame for war within is often laid to the charge of environments, when they come, as St. James says, from within. Of course there are many ways in the outer life through which it finds expression, but the real trouble is the lust within.

Can it be thought by any that have any knowledge of God and His plan of salvation that this is the very best which can be done for us? James 4:6, says: "He giveth more grace." Yea, to all such, let it be said that they need not live in this state of double-mindedness where the civil war rages forever.

II.   How may we be delivered? This is an important question, and one that we would hesitate to answer, were it not so plainly given in this same epistle.

1. Submission to God.

The apostle knew that this is the hardest victory to win. The carnal nature never likes to submit to another, and especially to God, for "it is enmity to God, and is not subject to the law of God, neither indeed can be." "God resisteth the proud, but giv-

eth grace to the humble.   Submit yourselves therefore to God" (James 4:6, 7).

When God can, with full consent of the human
heart, enter this citadel of man's being, He begins a
work that will tell in time and for eternity.   But
nothing can be done until God has the right of way.
To do this, our plans and opinions must be surrendered, if they are antagonistic to God's plans.   How
the personal pronoun "I" will go down under this
requirement!

2.   Resist the devil.

When this last ditch is being surrendered to God,
the enemy of all good will reinforce the carnal nature with all the army of hell to defeat the work of
cleansing.   To him we must learn to say an eternal
"No" that will be repeated all the way to the grave.
He knows that in the clean heart there is not an inch
of territory for his occupancy.   He knows that
henceforth all his attacks must be from without, with
no sympathy from within.   He will be willing to
compromise on anything short of full salvation.   He
will agree to repression, growth in grace, death-bed
sanctification or purgatorial cleansing, yea, anything,
to keep us out of the blessing of entire sanctification
here and now.

3.   "Draw nigh to God" (James 4:8).   Here is
the place for poor double-minded souls to come.   All
human effort to remove this carnal mind is a failure.   God alone can do this.   Any effort of our own
to cast it out is putting our trust in an arm of flesh.
It will do no good to accept God's plan theoretically;

for Satan knows that nothing short of an experimental getting to God will bring deliverance. It is a pity that the untold multitude of converted Christians have never learned that the removal of the carnal mind is a divine work, and that they must come to God, who alone hath power to cleanse the heart.

4. "Cleanse the hands" (James 4:8). "Hands" in the Bible stand for actual deeds, and in this place for actual sins. Who has not learned from bitter experience that to do wrong, either by committing forbidden sin or omitting commanded duty, is the common experience of converted people! Hence sinners are not asked to be holy, but "repent," while backsliders are exhorted to return unto the Lord. The experience of entire sanctification begins on the plane of a clearly justified experience, and not of an unpardoned sinner or a backslidden believer. If, since conversion, the believer has committed known wilful sin, or neglected plain duty, he needs pardon, and his hands are not clean. Hence the exhortation, or rather command, "Cleanse your hands, ye sinners."

The sin of the unsaved, either in the church or out, is the sin of transgression, while the sin of the double-minded, for the most part, is that of omission, but in either case it is sin; and to be delivered from either one or the other, or both, pardon must be sought and obtained.

If your hands are clean, then are you ready for the next step, which is—

5. Heart purity. "Purify your hearts, ye double-minded" (James 4:8).

Clearly does the apostle teach that a state of double-mindedness is a state of heart impurity, while on the other hand a clean heart has only the one single mind of Jesus in it. In the sense of self purification that is impossible.

The Ethiopian can not change his skin, nor the leopard his spots. But there is a sense in which this is true. Salvation in this higher sense is co-operative, as well as in conversion. Man's part and then God's. In justification, man repents and turns to God, then God forgives and regenerates. In full salvation, man consecrates and trusts, then God cleanses and fills with the Holy Ghost. Hence the Lord, by the mouth of Moses, said to Israel: "Sanctify yourselves therefore, and be ye holy. . . . I am the Lord which sanctify you" (Lev. 20:7, 8).

St. James shows that this is not a side issue, but adds: "Be afflicted, and mourn, and weep; let your laughter be turned to mourning, and your joy to heaviness. Humble yourselves in the sight of the Lord."

What a thorough work! No healing slightly the hurt of the daughter of Zion. Here is a going to the bottom, and an applying the balm of Gilead by the Great Physician that He may fulfil the promise succeeding these directions: "And he shall lift you up." O blessed lifting! O wonderful deliverance! Who that ever drank this cup of gall does not remember it? And then, when the cup of salvation, full and complete, is placed to the lips of the soul, and the poor thirsty one drinks of its sweets, can he ever forget it? How unthankful ever to forget or deny it.

If you are converted and not sanctified, your heart is not yet fully right with God, but in a state of transition. Do not stop when you get the mind of Christ, which you do in regeneration, but press on until the mind of Satan is taken out of you, which is done in entire sanctification.

SKETCH OF A SERMON ON DANCING.

The "sketch" of Rev. W. A. Dodge which follows is not only quite instructive, but indicates very
clearly how thoroughly he prepared his sermons.
The elaborateness of this one suggests a mind which
did not carry unbeaten oil into the sanctuary.   He
was no slovenly preacher, nor was he one who was
careless or negligent in preparing his sermons, trusting alone to the inspiration of the occasion for matter with which to fill up.   He was pointed, clear,
practical, coming down to the level on which people live.

When this sermon was preached we have no
means of knowing, but wherever the trumpet voice
of this man of God uttered it, we may be sure God
was in it, and it carried conviction and left lasting
impressions for good.   Here it is:

WHEN DANCING IS ALLOWED AND DISALLOWED.

Colossians 3 : 17 : "And whatsoever ye do in word
or deed, do all in the name of the Lord Jesus, giving thanks unto God and the Father by him."

I.   Introduction—Why preach on the subject?

II.   How can we expect to succeed?

III.   Three rules by which to judge when dancing
is right and when it is wrong:

1.   By the spirit which prompts it.

2.   The circumstances which attend it.

3.   The ends had in view in the indulgence: (1)
Is it for the glory of God? (2) Is it for our own

good—mental, moral and physical? (3) Is it for the good of the race?

IV. When is dancing allowable? Let us examine the Bible for the answer.

First instance—Miriam—Exodus 15:20, 21.

Second instance—David—11 Samuel 6:14.

Three facts appear in these two instances: 1. There was no complicity of the sexes. 2. There were no previous arrangements. 3. It was intended to praise God.

V. What sort of dancing is not allowable, and when is it not permissible?

1. When not done to the glory of God, or when it is the offspring of an unconverted heart—when done as an act of idolatry or to glorify men, and when the disastrous results show the Divine displeasure; as for instance:

(1) When Israel danced before the golden calf. Exodus 32:19.

(2) When David returned from the slaughter of the Philistines. 1 Samuel, 18:6, 7.

(3) When Herodias danced before Herod. Matthew, 14:6.

VI. Note the fruits of dancing. "By their fruits ye shall know them."

1. In a person under conviction for sin.

2. In a young convert.

VII. What the Church expects and has a right to demand of those who voluntarily join:

1. To abstain from all appearance of evil.

11 d

2. To obey the Scriptures.

Notice, then, the scriptural argument:

(1.) See 1 Corinthians, 10:31, 32. (2.) Colossians, 3:17. (3.) Obedience. Hebrews, 13:17. (4.) The General Rules, which forbids the doing of what we know is not for the glory of God. (5.) A "time to dance." (6.) See who are present on dancing occasions. (7.) It is no time to dance when you are not prepared to die.

(Here follows several illustrations of this point.)

VIII. The opinions of those who were not Christians, as well as the most religious people, are decidedly against dancing.

Here the preacher quoted from Cicero, Demosthenes, Ovid, St. Ambrose, Tertullian, St. Basil, Augustine, and John Wesley.

IX. Let us notice why the counsel of the ungodly should not be taken upon this mooted question:

1. Their knowledge of the Bible is too superficial. Instances—Ecclesiastes, 3:4. See the Prodigal Son.

2. The natural man can not receive the things of the Spirit.

3. They do not speak the truth when they talk of the benefits of the dance.

Note, for instance, these things: (1.) The costumes worn on such occasions. (2.) The place where dancing is indulged. (3.) The time wasted in the dance, and the late hours kept. (4.) The folly of claiming that it gives grace and manners.

X.   What shall be done to stop dancing?

1.   Let all who profess the name of Christ abstain from it.

2.   Let parents take the matter in hand.

3.   Let ministers speak out plainly against it.

4.   Let the laymen come to the help of the ministry.

XI.   A word to those who dance:

1.   Why do you dance?

(1.)   To find pleasure?   (2.)   To find company?

2.   By dancing you are wasting your precious life, and, worse than all, you are murdering your soul.

3.   By dancing, you increase your already over-fondness for dress and show.

4.   Stay away from it, for your parents are opposed to your dancing.

5.   It will—if it has not already done so—give you a distaste for God's Word, for prayer, and for self-examination.

————————

"Thus in thine arms of love, O God, I lie,
   Lost, and forever lost, to all but thee,
My happy soul, since it hath learned to die,
   Hath found new life in thine infinity.

"Oh, go and learn the lesson of the Cross,
   And tread thy way which saints and prophets
      trod,
Who, counting life and self and all things loss,
   Have found in inward death the life of God."

HANDWRITTEN CONSECRATION OF
W. A. DODGE

St Pauls Church. ¿ I this day make a full
Atlanta Ga. ¿ Consecration of all I have
and am to God. now hinceforth and forever
Myself.— My body. Eyes, Tongue, Hands, Feet.
Mind.— And Heart.— My. wife. Mary Dodge
My Child. Wisley Atkins Dodge. and my
Little daughter May Bell. Dodge.— My books
Clothes, Money, all I now have. and all
I ever expect to have. Yes all my means
are and shall be thine. My Time, &c

And if there is any thing else that appertains to me that I have not mentioned,
I lay it on Gods altar. to stay there
forever: I do this from a Conviction
of duty.— that all I have belongs to
by right to Him.— Not as a Compromise
—but from a sense of duty: Simply asking that I may be aided by him to Keep
it there.—

Signed sealed and delivered
in the this Sunday. at St Pauls Church April
15 = 1876 In the presence of Him who
sees all things, through the Sprit to Witness.

W. A. Dodge

This to Stay Sealed during my natural life
Monument of my Consecration to God.
April. 15 = 1876

REV. W. A. DODGE

Taken from *Yearbook and Minutes of the 38th Session, North Georgia Conference of M.E. Church, South, 1904*

William Asbury Dodge was born September 30, 1844, in Columbia County, GA, near Harlem, and departed this life January 16th, 1904, in East Point, GA, after a lingering illness, in which he suffered intensely. He was soundly converted before he was fourteen years of age, was licensed to exhort on his sixteenth birthday and licensed to preach on his seventeenth birthday. He entered the Georgia Conference in 1862, was a chaplain in the Confederate Army, and spent more than forty years in the ministry.

In 1862 he was first married to Miss Henrietta Williams, of Oxford, GA, who did not live very long thereafter. While he was on the Decatur Circuit, in 1867, she passed away. He was married the second time to Mrs. Mary Chandler, widow of Rev. W. B. Chandler, a local preacher, December 2nd, 1869, of DeKalb County, GA. Four children were born unto them, three of whom survive.

As to what he was, let others who knew him speak:

The *Wesleyan Christian Advocate* in noticing his death said: "He was cheerful, active, robust, and from the date of entering the Conference, was effective and an efficient Methodist minister. He was a good preacher, scriptural, sensible, strong and had rare gifts as a revivalist, and many souls through his ministry have been led to Christ and established in their religious lives."

Rev. George G. Smith says: "He ought to have been good. He had good parentage. His mother was a superior woman, of deep religious character. His father belonged to the sturdy New England stock which gave the great philanthropist, Wm. E. Dodge, to the world. He lived up to his profession for thirty years and never wavered in his adherence to his position, that there is a distinct second work of grace, called entire sanctification, to be reached now by faith instantaneously, and he became a leader in the movement which sought to further the work of holiness. Warm-hearted, benevolent, hospitable, upright, always ready for every good work, he had the full confidence of all who knew him. The godless recognized him as a good man who aimed all the time to lift up and comfort and direct in the right way. He was full of the Holy Spirit. It was his religion that made him good. He had learned much of the Divine Spirit, and of that gracious benediction called the fullness of God, and religion to him was an abiding thing, and not something intermittent. The crowning fruit of this Spirit's indwelling is love, and his great heart overflowed with it. Toward his Holiness brethren whom he believed were advocating and seeking to advance what he believed to be the highest truth, his heart went out in constant love, but towards all the Good Spirit made him affectionate, tolerant and kind. He was a true exemplar of the fruits of the Spirit, meek, patient, gentle, faithful, he always had a well spring of joy within. He was no time server, no conformer with anybody, nor anything in the matter of duty. He might have been mistaken as to what was right, but what he saw was true he was ready to die for. He fully believed the power of the Gospel he preached. He was a great evangelist. He expected souls to be converted and Christians to be sanctified, and the fullness of his faith led him to dare great things and expect great things. He believed that God was willing to save sinners, and it was the most natural thing that they should be saved. Dear, warm-hearted Dodge! How sadly we will miss him."

Brother Dodge thus speaks in some of his writings, of his religious experience after his conversion: "In the fall of 1876, the second year of my pastorate at St. Paul's, Atlanta, my heart began to hunger for the blessings of entire sanctification. After earnest prayer for more than one hour, the Holy Spirit brought to my remembrance Hebrews 7:25, 'Wherefore He is able to save them to the uttermost that come unto God by Him, seeing He ever liveth to make intercession for them.' I immediately said: Yes, there is a full salvation. I see it. He is my utmost Saviour and my Keeper, too, and in a moment the storm was over, and the sweetest calm came into my soul. The work was done. I claim the blessing and the keeping. On my way home, the Spirit said: 'Now will you tell it?' Satan said: 'What wilt your brethren say about it?' Then this passage came to my mind: John 5:44, 'How can ye believe which receive honor one of another, and seek not the honor that cometh from God only?' If they turn me out of the Church, I must and will confess what He hath done for my soul." This was April 15th, 1876, at St. Paul's Church.

For twenty-eight years he enjoyed this rich religious experience, never doubting it for once, and humbly confessing it before men, and faithfully exemplified it to them.

Rev. W. H. Lloyd, formerly of the South Georgia Conference, has this to say: "He was one of the purest, sweetest spirited men that our Methodism has given to the world. He was truly a man who put his whole soul into his work. He was no self-seeker, nor was he ever triflingly employed. With all his earnest advocacy of entire sanctification, he never ignored, nor abused the Church, but on the contrary, co-operated in all her missionary, Church extension, and other benevolent enterprises to the fullest extent."

His brethren who labored with him know this is true in every particular. At the time of his death he was the faithful and efficient Treasurer of the Board of Church Extension, and no man was truer to this interest of the Church. His place was hard to fill.

With all his earnest advocacy of what he believed to be the Wesleyan view of holiness, he was tolerant of others, and no man can rise up and say he ever showed the slightest disloyalty to the Church of his choice, nor that he ever gave any encouragement whatever to division or schism. He loved the Methodist Church, was true to his ordination vows, and gave the best part of his life to her ministry, ever going cheerfully without question where he was sent.

The life of this good man was far from being free from trials peculiar to the life of a Methodist itinerant. He was an excellent pastor, and sought to be true to the discipline of the Church. At one of his appointments, dancing had taken root among the membership and Brother Dodge endeavored to administer judicious discipline at the time. As every preacher knows who has had to do this strange work, it is not pleasant, and he sought advice from Bishop Pierce, who writes him a very tender and touching letter now preserved, in which this noble man encouraged him in the course he was pursuing, and heartily endorsed him in seeking to rid the Church of dancing members.

The last hours of our departed and now glorified brother were full of thrilling interest. No terror of death was there. His death was one of the most triumphant, just such a death as we would have supposed Asbury Dodge to have died. On Thursday night before he left this world for the good world he said to Rev. G. W. Matthews, one of his most intimate friends, as he went into the room to greet the dying man: "George, I am almost in heaven."

Calmly he viewed his approaching end, and said he believed God wanted him to go then—that he had prayed ever since God had given him children that he might live to see them grown and settled, and God had graciously granted his request, and he believed wanted him to go now. For four months preceding his departure for the skies, his prayer every day at family prayer was, "Lord, prepare us all for what Thou art preparing for us." His wife thought that the prayer had particular reference to his next Conference appointment, but after Conference it was the same prayer. So when the last hour came, and his family had to give him up, then it was seen for what he had been so constantly praying, and that for which his Father had been preparing him.

When his ransomed spirit left the tenement of clay, for several minutes there was not a tear shed, for it seemed to those present that the very room was filled with the presence of angels.

Just before he breathed his last, his devoted and afflicted wife, holding him by the hand, asked him if he felt that the Lord Jesus was still with him. He bowed his head a moment, and promptly answered, "Yes, and He has been with me all the time." Showing deep interest in and concern for the wife of his bosom, he would forget himself, and when he would see a tear in her eye he would lift his hand and say, "Don't, don't."

His home life was indeed beautiful, and his devotion to the good woman who had so long stood by his side, the partner of his joys and sorrows, and the companion of his toils and travels, was indeed touching. Fourteen months before he died, his wife met with an accident in Rome, which made her an invalid for life, and she necessarily required much of his time and attention. No husband could have been more careful and attentive, and never for one moment did he ever grow weary in waiting upon and caring for her in her suffering and helplessness.

His wife bears testimony to this tender care and sincere devotion, for she says that during these long weary months he nursed her as if she were a baby. Once she said, "Mr. Dodge, don't you ever get tired?" and he quickly replied, "No, as long as you keep sweet, I will never get tired."

To her he would frequently repeat the precious promises of God's word, such as, "My grace is sufficient for thee," "Cast thy burdens upon the Lord and He will sustain thee," "I can do all things through Christ which strengtheneth me," while the last Scripture uttered by him, just before he went away to come back no more, was, "The blood of Jesus Christ, thy Son, cleanseth us from all sin."

He was fully aware his end was near, and acted as if he was just going away on a journey. About an hour before he died, he called his loved ones to him and bade them a final and affectionate farewell. He bade his loving and devoted wife good-bye, then drew her down into his arms in an affectionate embrace, and then each one of his children, whom he embraced and bade farewell in turn, then at last, Wesley, the faithful colored man, who had been with the family for nearly twenty years, came for the final farewell, and he, too, was clasped by the dying, triumphant man of God, to whom death had no sting and grave no victory. And thus he left them to meet them again in heaven, whither he has gone. With his benediction falling upon those about his dying couch, he gathered up his feet, and quietly fell asleep in Jesus, just outside the gates of the celestial city, to awake the next moment in the home of the good.

CLEMENT C. CARY

Conference History of Rev. W. A. Dodge:

November, 1862, admitted on trial; 1863, Watkinsville Circuit, junior; 1864-65, Chaplain in the Army; January, 1865, Ordained Deacon by Bishop Pierce; 1866-67-68, Decatur; December, 1866, Ordained Elder by Bishop McTyiere; 1869, Atlanta City Mission; 1870, Evans Chapel and Mission, Atlanta; 1871, Dahlonega; 1872-73, Presiding Elder Dahlonega District; 1874, Presiding Elder Gainesville District; 1875-76, St. Paul, Atlanta; 1877-78, Sparta; 1879-80-81-82, Eatonton; 1883, Atlanta City Mission; 1884, Boulevard and Exposition Mills Mission, Atlanta; 1885, Gainesville; 1886, Cartersville; 1887, Fulton Circuit; 1888 Supernumerary; 1889, Record does not show; 1890, Forsyth Circuit; 1891, Bolton; 1892, Conference Colporteur; 1893, Walker Street, Atlanta; 1894, South Atlanta Mission; 1895, Supernumerary; 1896, Supernumerary; 1897, Supernumerary; 1898, East Point; 1899, East Point; 1900, East Point; 1991, East Point; 1992, Second Church, Rome; 1993, St. James, Atlanta; 1994, Fairburn.

OBITUARY OF REV. W. A. DODGE

Taken from *THE PENTECOSTAL HERALD*

Wednesday, February 3, 1904

REV. WILLIAM ASBURY DODGE

A TRIBUTE BY REV. W. O. BUTLER, PASTOR OF ST. JAMES CHURCH, ATLANTA, GA.

After a protracted illness of two months or more, in which great physical pain was patiently endured, the triumphant spirit of this noble soldier of the cross took its flight to a realm where there is no more sickness nor death, but where sorrow and sighing shall flee away and where there shall be no more pain.

At four o'clock, Saturday afternoon, January 16th, while gloomy clouds overcast the skies and the rain was falling, death came to him at East Point and set free his conquering soul into the world that the eagle eye of faith had before explored, when, on beatific vision, it had roamed amid the hilltops of glory. With his loved ones about his bedside—his invalid wife, his son, W. A. Dodge, Jr., his two sweet daughters, Miss Mae Belle, and Mrs. W. T. Callahan—with his benedictions falling upon them, he gathered up his feet in death and fell asleep just outside the gates of glory.

BEDSIDE SCENE—About an hour before he died, Bro. Dodge called his loved ones to him and bade them farewell. He bade his loving wife good-bye, and drew her down into his arms in affectionate embrace; and then his children, all of whom he fondly embraced. Then Wesley, the faithful colored man, who had been with the family nearly twenty years, came for a final farewell, and he, too, was clasped in the embrace of the dying Christian. And thus he left us, demonstrating that divine love that is as large as the planet on which we live.

THE FUNERAL—Monday, January 18th, at Walker Street Methodist Church, Atlanta, of which he was once the beloved pastor, the funeral services were held, amid the love and tears and beautiful floral tributes of a large circle of friends. The auditorium was so covered with people eager to do him honor, that a large number stood during the entire proceedings. The Scripture lesson was read by Rev. John H. Lashburn, pastor of Walker St. Church; prayer was offered by Rev. Dr. C. E. Dowman, Presiding Elder of the Atlanta District, and the sermon was by Rev. Geo. W. Matthews, Presiding Elder of the Dublin District, South Georgia Conference, one of the most intimate friends of Brother Dodge. The songs and music were arranged and rendered by Charlie D. Tillman, also one of his dear friends, assisted by his venerable father, Rev. Jas. L. Tillman; and his little daughter Jewel Dodge Tillman, who, with touching pathos, sang "The City of Gold" and "Jesus Knows and Jesus Cares."

THE SERMON—The sermon by Bro. Matthews was a review of the laborious, self-denying, successful and saintly life of his deceased friend, not leaving out the connection of Brother Dodge with the holiness movement in Georgia and in the South. The speaker fervently spoke of the devotion of the deceased to duty and his loyalty to his convictions as to the teachings of his church on the subject of entire sanctification, and of his courage in maintaining those doctrines in the face of any opposition or persecution or loss that might come to him in their advocacy. The preacher showed that Bro. Dodge was not only true to his convictions and experience as to doctrine, but was to the core loyal to the M. E. Church, South, and would not listen with favor to any proposition or solicitation that came to him from other communions, freighted with promises of higher places and larger salary. Whatever of talent, or power, or ability he might have had, he had consecrated to the church he loved, and had determined it should remain so to the end.

THE FINAL SCENE—After the sermon there were many brief talks from ministers (of which there were more than forty present) and laymen, as to Brother Dodge's exalted Christian character and eminent usefulness as preacher, pastor, altar-worker and evangelist. A large concourse looked upon the peaceful marble face and then the funeral cortege slowly wended its way to the shades of Oakland, where the body waits until it shall be glorified by the resurrection power of the Son of God.

LIFE SKETCH—Rev. W. A. Dodge was born September 30, 1845. (Compiler's Note: this date should be 1944.) Entered the Georgia Conference in 1862, spending more than forty years in the work of the ministry. He served on missions, circuits, stations, and as editor and presiding elder.

In all these fields he was found faithful and successful. He was eminently a revivalist and soul-winner, and was noted as an altar worker the peer of any. It was while he was pastor of St. Paul's Church in Atlanta, in 1879, (Compiler's Note: this date should be 1876.) that he entered into the experience of entire sanctification. Here his ardent soul found free exercise in leading hundreds of hungry souls into the same joyous and fruitful life. In connection with his now sainted comrades, Rev. A. J. Jarrell and Rev. W. C. Dunlap, Brother Dodge was the founder and promoter of the now famous Indian Springs Holiness Campground, where thousands annually go for help on spiritual lines. The camp-meetings he greatly enjoyed, and the successful promulgation of holiness there was one of his chief delights. Such was his love for that consecrated spot, that he said something in his last illness about being buried amid its hallowed groves and sacred scenes. But not only in Georgia did he preach holiness successfully, but also his clarion voice was heard in the camps and churches of Texas, Arkansas, Tennessee, Kentucky, North and South Carolina, Missouri and other States, calling sinners to repentance, and the Church to a higher experience and holy life. Let us follow him as he followed Christ, and meet him among the angels.

W. A. Dodge

THE HOLINESS MOVEMENT IN THE SOUTH

Taken From *THE PENTECOSTAL HERALD*
Date?

By Rev. W. A. Dodge

Dr. Lovick Pierce, the father of Bishop Geo. F. Pierce, was the nestor of the holiness movement in the South. He obtained the experience while assisting Dr. Hamilton in the city of Mobile, Ala., in 1842. For years he did his best to push the work into a great movement, but the great question of slavery was up, which resulted the division of the church, North and South. It then began to take on a national failure which resulted in the Civil War that divided and embittered the people until it became manifest that the public heart was not ready for a great work like this. The results of the war left our people with a spirit in them not very friendly to the holiness movement. Thousands have never touched it for the reason that they said it came from beyond Mason's and Dixon's line. So the old gentleman let it run down to what he called a "closet experience." Thus things remained until about the year 1876, when a brother Ludlow, from Newark, N.J., on a trip South, met the now sainted Rev. A. J. Jarrell, who was then pastor of St. James' M. E. Church, South, Augusta, Ga. They soon became fast friends. Mr. L. extorted from Bro. Jarrell the promise that he would make him a visit to his New Jersey home, which promise was kept, and came off during a great holiness camp-meeting at Ocean Grove, N. J., where the now sainted John S. Inskip had a home, and was in charge of the meetings.

This meeting was used of God in the sanctification of Bro. Jarrell. His new experience was so sweet that he desired to see his people come into it. It was not long before his intense desire resulted in an engagement with Dr. Inskip to come to Georgia and hold a meeting for him in St. James, Augusta.

The following fall he came, and under God a work of grace resulted that was a benediction. The Doctor held a meeting in Trinity, Charleston, S. C., another in Trinity, Savannah, Ga. These meetings were seasons of power. A new life came into the pew and pulpit all over the land.

Soon the preachers and laymen began to feel that the need was other meetings on the same line.

Rev. G. H. Pattillo, then stationed at Milledgeville, Ga. opened his church and initiated one to be held there.

The next year one was held in Griffin, Ga., Dr. Jas. E. Evans, pastor. The following spring Rev. A. J. Jarrell, then stationed in Gainesville, Ga., invited the brethren and friends to concentrate there. Dr. Geo. D. Watson, then stationed in Newport, Ky., was invited to come and do the preaching. Such preaching we had never heard. O, how the Spirit did own and bless it to the awakening of the people. We saw things there that beggar all description.

It was during this meeting that the North Georgia Holiness Association was organized, with Rev. A. J. Jarrell as President, Rev. W. C. Dunlap, Vice-President, and Rev. W. A. Dodge, Secretary and Treasurer.

In the mean time it became manifest that some means of communication was a necessity. After several conferences between a few interested, the "Way of Life" was launched. It was a small sheet of four pages, with Rev. W. A. Dodge as editor. The demand soon became so great for space that it had to be enlarged to a six-column quarto. It was soon seen that once a month was not often enough. Then it was sent out twice a month. The work continued to grow until the demand was for a weekly. At one time it was the only organ in the South on this distinctive line.

It dawned upon those pushing the work that our people must read if they would be intelligent on the doctrine. The cry was for books. The demand at first was for inexpensive books, but as the work spread there was a demand for larger and more expensive works. These at first had to be secured in other markets. But as time went by, the Spirit seemed to come on our own people to write. The first was a small booklet by Dr. W. B. Godbey, called "Full Salvation." Then his "Sanctification." Following this was his little book called "Christian Perfection." After this his "Holiness or Hell," "Victory," "Woman Preacher," and now his commentaries. The Spirit came upon Dr. B. Carradine and he began to write, until he has a book for each year of his evangelistic ministry.

Then the need for song-books. So the Spirit began to inspire among us men and women to write songs and set them to music. Out of this has come "Revival" Nos. 1 and 2, while a third is now soon to be out. These are by a man in the experience. "Cheerful Songs," "Tears and Triumphs," and quite a number of small books have flooded the country.

By this time other papers on this line were being sent all over the land. "The Way of Faith,"The Revival," "Old Methodist," afterward called the "Kentucky Methodist" later it was known as "The Methodist and Way of Life," but now the "PENTECOSTAL HERALD." Later the "Tennessee Methodist,"which has changed its heading to the "Outlook."

All this has not been done without opposition. Satan is too smart to let a work like this go on without an effort on his part to stop it. So he began early to thwart it. He has used instrumentalities that often surprise us; but what cares he so he may destroy the work. He has printed books, published papers, legislated, all to put an end to it. All sorts of measures have been adopted, fair and foul, true and false to stop it—but on it goes.

We are now in the camp-meeting stage of the movement. Scottsville, Texas, is the mother of them all. These places dot our Southland from Virginia to Texas; from the Everglades in Florida to the Ohio river.

Men and women under the baptism of the Holy Spirit have come forth by the score to preach and testify to this Bible doctrine. If we would begin to tell of them we would not be able to tell of their names, sufferings and success. God bless them. Their names are in the Book of Life.

OBITUARY OF MRS. W. A. DODGE

DODGE – Mrs. Mary Etta Dodge, widow of Rev. W. A. Dodge, died February 4, 1920, in her eightieth year, in East Point, Ga., at the home of her daughter, Mrs. Annie Callahan, with whom for many years she has made her home.

She was the daughter of Zachariah and Mary Jones, born in DeKalb County, Georgia, June 2, 1840. In early girlhood she was converted and joined the Methodist Church. She and Rev. Mr. Chandler married in 1857, to whom was born a child, who died in infancy. He died in 1862, having been a chaplain in the Confederate army.

December 2, 1869, at the old home, she and Rev. W. A. Dodge were married, to whom were born four children. One died in infancy. Mabel, a noble Christian young woman, left earth for heaven ten years ago. Surviving her are a son, W. Atticus Dodge, of Atlanta, and a daughter, Mrs. Anna Callahan, of East Point, Ga.

These are the material facts in the life of this excellent Christian woman. Marrying an itinerant Methodist preacher, she was never a hindrance to him, but entered heartily and sympathetically into all his work. It was indeed a congenial couple, both well mated, one the helper of the other. His life and trials were hers and cheerfully she moved as he was appointed to his several charges. No complaint could ever have been lodged against her as the wife of a Methodist preacher.

Quietly and in contentment she spent her last days, always cheerful and hopeful, with a simple, childlike faith in her Lord and Savior. Her excellent qualities and her sweet, Christian spirit drew people to her. She was deeply interested in Indian Springs Camp Meeting, for her husband had much to do with founding that noted institution. It was her great delight to attend the annual meetings at that consecrated place.

She was fully aware of her approaching end, and no harrowing fears haunted her mind nor disturbed the quietude of her soul. But going away was quietly arranged, and she made all her plans and told her children just what she wanted done. In less than an hour of her departure she inquired of her daughter concerning a niece who had been with her that day, and told her she had better go home before it was dark.

October 10, 1902, while her husband was at Second Church, Rome, she had her hip broken in an unfortunate street car accident, and the doctor said she would never get out of bed. But she was tenderly nursed by her devoted husband as if she had been a child, and constant prayer was made for her. To the surprise of every one, on December 6, she was moved to East Point, Ga., and finally so far recovered as to walk wherever she desired. She and her husband firmly believed her recovery was due to prayer. She suffered much after this, yet no complaint ever escaped her lips. She was God's child and in His hands and what He did with her was all right.

Peacefully and with a good hope of the future, she fell asleep just as a child would in its mother's arms, and woke in Heaven. It was a glad meeting on the other shore when W. A. Dodge greeted the wife of his bosom whom he had to leave on earth in January, 1904, and when that sweet spirit of Mabel Dodge met her sainted and disembodied mother. What a happy time they have been having since that day in February of this year as this trio have roamed the fair fields of Eden! We will see them all again.

Clement C. Cary

RESOLUTIONS

Of the Woman's Missionary Society of East Point
Methodist Church, South.

DODGE —Whereas, our kind Heavenly Father, in His wisdom, has seen fit to take to her heavenly home our beloved friend and sister, Mrs. Mary Jones Dodge, God saw it was enough for she had served untiringly and He took her to that land where weary saints find a sweet rest. Therefore be it.

Resolved first, That our Woman's Missionary Society and our entire community have sustained a great loss in giving up this one whose life was so beautiful and influence so wonderful.

Resolved second, That we cherish her memory in our hearts and in our daily walk strive to live up to that high ideal of life that was hers.

Resolved third, That a copy of these resolutions be sent to her family, accompanied by our sincere sympathy.

Resolved fourth, That a copy be sent to the *Wesleyan Christian Advocate* and that we also inscribe them on our minutes.

Mrs. C. A. Norton,

Mrs. J. R. Campbell,

Mrs. W. H. Caldwell,

Miss Emma Harrison.

A SELECT BIBLIOGRAPHY

Brasher, J. Lawrence. *The Sanctified South, John L. Brasher and the Holiness Movement*. Urbana: University of Illinois Press, 1994.

Brown, Kenneth O. *Indian Springs Holiness Camp Meeting, A History of "The Greatest Camp Meeting in the South."* Hazleton: Holiness Archives, 2000.

Brown, Kenneth O. *Inskip, McDonald, Fowler: "Wholly and Forever Thine," Early Leadership in the National Camp Meeting Association for the Promotion of Holiness*. Hazleton: Holiness Archives, 1999.

Butler, Rev. W. G. "Rev. William Asbury Dodge," in *The Pentecostal Herald*, February 3, 1904, p. 8. [Tribute of Reverend William A. Dodge.]

Cary, Rev. C. C. "From North Georgia," in *The Pentecostal Herald*, February 10, 1904, p. 2. [Memorial article about Rev. William A. Dodge.]

_____. "Mrs. Mary Etta Dodge," undated article in the "Dodge Scrapbook."

Dayton, Donald W. *Theological Roots of Pentecostalism*. Peabody: Hendrickson Publishers, 1991.

Dieter, Melvin E. *The Holiness Revival of the Nineteenth Century*. Metuchen: Scarecrow Press, 1980

"Dodge, William Asbury," in *Minutes of the Annual Conference of the Methodist Episcopal Church, South*. Nashville: Publishing House of the Methodist Episcopal Church, South, 1904, pp. 152-154. [Conference memoir.]

Dodge, Rev. W. A. "The Holiness Movement in the South," in *The Pentecostal Herald*, December 14, 1898, p. 6. [Historical article by W. A. Dodge.]

Garbutt, Mrs. J. W. *Rev. W. A. Dodge as We Knew Him: With Sketches of His Life, Diary, Consecration and Sermons*. Atlanta: Franklin Printing and Publishing Co., 1906.

Jernigan, Rev. C. B. *Pioneer Days of the Holiness Movement in the Southwest*. Kansas City: Pentecostal Nazarene Publishing House, 1919.

Johnson, Z. T. *The Story of Indian Springs Holiness Camp*. Flovilla: 1965.

Jones, Charles Edwin. *Perfectionist Persuasion: The Holiness Movement and American Methodism, 1867-1936*. ATLA Monograph Series, no. 5. Metuchen: The Scarecrow Press, 1974

Matthews, Annie. *Our Golden Anniversary: A Retrospect of Fifty Years of the Indian Springs Holiness Camp Meeting*. No publishing data, 1940.

_____. *Memorial Stones: Spiritual Epochs in the Lives of George and Annie Matthews*. Atlanta: 1945. [Reprinted by the Francis Asbury Society, Wilmore, KY, 1999.]

Matthews, Rev G. W. "The Movement in Georgia; a study of the faults and virtues of distinctive holiness work." Columbia, SC: *Way of Faith*, 1914.

Middlebrooks, Frances Hughes. *Echoes of Camp Meeting: A Centennial Review, Indian Springs Holiness Camp Ground, 1890-1990*. Winter Park: Wicks Printing, 1890.

Minnix, Kathleen. *Laughter in the Amen Corner, The Life of Evangelist Sam Jones*. Athens: The University of Georgia Press, 1993.

Pierce, Alfred M. *A History of Methodism in Georgia*. Published by the North Georgia Conference Historical Society, 1956.

Rose, Delbert R. *Vital Holiness: A Theology of Christian Experience*. Minneapolis: Bethany Fellowship, 1975

Smith, Timothy L. *Called Unto Holiness: The Story of the Nazarenes*. Kansas City: Nazarene Publishing House, 1962.

Turley, Briane K. "A Wheel Within a Wheel: Southern Methodism and the Georgia Holiness Association," a Ph.D. dissertation submitted to the University of Virginia, 1994.

Turley, Briane K. "A Wheel Within a Wheel: Southern Methodism and the Georgia Holiness Association," in *Georgia Historical Quarterly*, Summer, 1991.

Turley, Briane K. *A Wheel Within a Wheel: Southern Methodism and the Georgia Holiness Association*. Macon: Mercer University Press, 1999.